WHY
PEOPLE
BUY

By Guy E. Baker CLU, MSFS

 STANDEL PUBLISHING

Printed in the United States

ISBN 0-9647721-0-8

Third Printing

Table Of Contents

About The author

Guy Baker is Managing Director of BTA Advisory Group, a Newport Beach, California based management consulting firm specializing in the issues and problems facing closely held businesses. He is also the Managing Director of Baker, Thomsen Associates, a compensation and benefits consulting firm specializing in closely-held businesses.

Guy graduated from Claremont McKenna College (BS/Economics-1967) and the University of Southern California (MBA Finance-1968). Guy earned a Chartered Life Underwriter (CLU) degree in 1972 and Chartered Financial Consultant degree in 1981. He also holds a Master's degree in Financial Services (MSFS) and Master's degree in Management (MSM). In addition, he is a Certified Financial Planner (CFP), and a Registered Health Underwriter (RHU).

In addition to being a life and qualifying member of the Million Dollar Round Table [MDRT] since 1970, he has been a continuing member of the Top of the Table (the top 500 international agents) since 1977. Guy has received many industry awards, including the Pacific Mutual's Preston Hotchkis Distinguished Service Award, Agent of the Year and the Orange County Agent of the Year. He led the Pacific Mutual agency field force in total production for seven years since 1986. He also finished as one of their top ten agents for over 20 consecutive years. He was admitted to their Council of Leaders in 1995.

Guy is active in the community, currently serving as Chairman of the Mexican Christian Missions in San Diego, an organization which supports over 60 churches and pastors throughout Mexico. He is also Chairman of the Board of Regents for the Instituto Internationale Biblico de Mexico. He was a major gifts fund-raiser for the Orange County Center for Performing Arts and has also served on the fund raising committee for South Coast Repertory Theater. He is Past President of the Claremont McKenna Alumni Association and was a member of CMC's Board of Trustees.

An internationally known speaker, Guy wrote *Baker's Dozen— 13 Principles for Financial Success.* His booklet, *The BOX,* has been widely distributed by life agents as an easy-to-understand discussion tool about the fundamentals of life insurance. He has just finished his 8 cassette training album called "Market Tune-up" to assist professionals in increasing their productivity.

Guy has been married to Colleen since 1967 and they live in San Juan Capistrano. They have four children and five grandchildren.

Introduction

When I first told my mother I was going into life insurance sales, I thought she was going to have a major stroke or heart attack right there on the spot. She had always thought I should be an attorney or an accountant or maybe a banker. But no! I had to go into life insurance sales. This was not a happy moment in our relationship.

When I first started selling, I dreamed of a secure job—one where I didn't have the pressure of always selling something. It wasn't until several years later that I truly understood that everybody is selling something most of the time. They are either selling their services, the reputation of the organization or a specific product. Selling is a natural part of any business relationship. Somebody is always selling and there always has to be somebody buying.

That is exactly why I decided to write this book. People buy, but why? Why do they buy from this particular company or person. What are the magic words, the catalyst, the motivation. If the selling side of the sales equation can harness the power of motivation, then the seller can achieve the sales success he desires.

A benefit of writing this book, that really surprised me, was the amount of interest people have in the whole subject of selling. When I first started talking about beginning this project, I had people ask me to send them a copy. If I mention this book whenever I give speeches on various sales subjects, I always get questions and inquiries. I particularly have found that attorneys and accountants are interested in *why people buy*.

Now, as you read this book, I hope you are not disappointed when you discover that I am not a formula type of guy. After 30 years of selling, I don't rely on power phrases and motivational thoughts to make the sale. I discovered a basic truth about selling years ago. I share this truth in the first chapter and it is the *core* of my sales philosophy. Once you grasp the power of this concept, you can become a master salesperson. There is nothing that can prevent you from achieving your sales goals. Once you embrace this concept the sky is the limit.

I make this promise to anyone who reads *Why People Buy*. If you don't get at least one good idea from this book, I will refund the cost of the book, no questions asked. It is the policy of our company to always have satisfied customers.

I am excited to have finished writing this book and published it so quickly. It took me almost ten years to do my first book, *Baker's Dozen*. It took nearly one year to do my second book, *The BOX*. *Why People Buy* only took two months. I bet I can do the next one in a month. However, I'm not ready to try yet.

I hope you have fun reading this book. Let me suggest one thought. I am sharing my selling system. It works for me, but it might not work for you. When I first started selling, I tried to be Ben Feldman, the person reputed to be the world's greatest life insurance salesman, one week. Then I tried being Mehdi the next week. After that it was Joe or Lyle, or whoever I was reading that month.

It wasn't until I decided to be Guy that I started to achieve any meaningful results. I had so successfully hidden the real me that I had no idea who I was. It wasn't until I came out from behind that mask and decided that if they didn't like who I was, then tough. I was just me. I did my best to do what I do best, teach. I simplified the complexities and helped people understand that my concepts could be beneficial to them.

I believe people buy from me because they trust that I will do what is right. But I also allow them the space to do what "they know is right." So when you read this, regardless of what level of success you have already achieved, regardless of what field of financial services you may be in, regardless of whether you are transactional or consultative, remember always to do what is right.

People buy you first and your product or service second. You know the old saying, *"they don't care what you know, until they know that you care."* It is my hope that you can use the contents of this book to help communicate your caring and your concern.

I want to thank Ken Harris for his help in making this book more interesting to read. Ken has been a big help to us as we have developed many of our training products. I'd like to thank Jill Boocock for her dedicated effort and personal time spent editing this masterpiece. Also, thanks to Becky Mahan for her energy and efforts towards improving this book. They are both wonderful helpers and have made what I write readable. A special thanks to Ralph Brown, my 30 year mentor. Ralph demonstrated to me early in my career that I could be successful selling life insurance. I think he now believes he has created a monster. But Ralph kept telling me I could do it and encouraged me when I was down.

I'd like to thank Colleen, my wife. She has had to endure many hours of clicking and tapping while I spun words onto my computer. But especially, I'd like to thank her for allowing me the freedom to pursue a selling career. She has made many sacrifices while I chased the golden ring. She has shared the ups and downs of commission living. She has been my partner in life since 1967. I suspect she'll hear a lot more clicking before I am through.

Finally, I'd like to thank the many people who have had the courage to buy from me during the years. I have enjoyed serving everybody I have ever had the privilege of helping secure their family's financial future. I just hope they feel the same way. Thank you one and all.

Now on with the show.

CHAPTER ONE

Perfect Practice Makes Perfect

ommission sales is really one of the last bastions of free enterprise left in the world. It is true capitalism at work. It works on the principle of supply and demand, the natural competition between a *willing* seller and a *wary* buyer. As a 30-year survivor of the "sales game," I can speak with some authority about its virtue and failings. As a sales trainer, I can tell you I have discovered that most sales professionals are woefully prepared when it comes to explaining why people buy.

I have developed my niche in the life insurance business. Many will say that if you can sell life insurance successfully, you can sell virtually anything. I don't know whether that is true or not. But I do know I was very successful selling shoes, sporting goods, and other consumer products before I went into insurance. This experience taught me that that there are repeatable patterns of buying behavior which we can learn to identify. I refer to these repeatable patterns as the selling process; a process that produces predictable results.

Think of a successful manufacturing company. The ones I have observed use a repeatable fabrication or manufacturing process when they assemble their widgets. Imagine if you will, the manager of the plant saying to the foreman, "Gee, how shall we do the process today?" I don't think so! What would happen to productivity and profit if the plant manager had to rethink and re-engineer the manufacturing process every day? Not only would the employees become confused, the quality of the product undoubtedly would suffer.

The point is, no organization can afford to start over each day. They have to have repeatable assembly and manufacturing processes that are time proven and tested. In fact, what happens is the time testing actually improves the manufacturing process. New ideas, efficiency improvements and new technology all result in economic improvements which ultimately increase productivity and profit. But implementing them takes study and thought.

I believe the same thing is true for salespeople. Regardless of the industry we represent, we also need a repeatable process that can be duplicated time and time again. We need a process that is time-tested and proven—one that can be practiced and improved as new ideas, technology and better understanding of human behavior come into being. All of these considerations increase efficiency and effectiveness.

It would be very difficult to ignore the processes of a professional athletes and the tremendous monetary success they have achieved in recent years. But only the best are rewarded. Imagine a top golfer or baseball player who walks out to perform without practicing, thinking, "Well, I'll just go out and see how I'll do." The stories are legendary about the hours Jack Nicklaus, Arnold Palmer, and Lee Trevino devoted to swinging the various clubs to work on tempo, form, feel and technique. They honed their skills with many hours of practice.

What happens when they don't practice? What happens when they layoff for a while? They have to play themselves back into form. Athletes coming off the disabled list take weeks before they gain their original form. Very little separates the *Haves* from the *Have Nots*. Yet, professional salespeople are not likely to be found practicing. And even if they did want to practice, what would they practice? That's what this book is all about, developing a process that you can learn and practice.

I started in the insurance business in 1966. I was taught a sales track that was written for the college market. I had a presentation booklet that followed the track. I called this my "Dick and Jane" reader. It had big words that were queued to the story line. I can still remember it today:

> "After years of experience, Pacific Mutual Life has found there are three very important factors for today's college student to consider when he starts thinking about his life insurance program. These factors are need, ability and in-surability? Does a man in college need life insurance?"

There was a lot more to the sales process than a memorized sales track. But the fact that I can still remember this sales spiel 30 years later, is testimony to the fact that I worked at it. I am not suggesting you need to memorize every word you are going to say to a prospective client, but I do believe that salespeople need to have a specific track to run on and they need to know it cold.

I decided to write this book so I could communicate what I have learned about selling. I have sold financial products for 30 years. I mentioned I have also sold shoes, sporting goods, cameras, stationary and hardware. I worked behind a hamburger counter, was a waiter (and dishwasher.) I believe the selling process is virtually the same, regardless of what you are selling—shoes, automobiles, hamburgers, durable goods, whatever.

There is a proven axiom of selling. *"People do what they want to do when they want to do it."* This is an important ingredient in understanding human behavior. If it is true, then as sales people, we are merely facilitators, not manipulators. Our job is to educate, to communicate what we have learned and know to be accurate, in a way that is appealing and informative. Once the buyer understands what we are saying, he will then ultimately decide what it is he wants to do.

There will certainly always be the impulse buyer—the buyer who makes a quick decision and then begins to question his or her wisdom after the fact. But do you want to build your career on finding those people? If the buyer's remorse is too high, even the impulse buyer will return the product or stop paying the annual fee. It is a fact of consumerism that the impulse buyer can rescind the transaction.

It's obvious, isn't it, that you are wasting your time if you have to reverse the sale. The advantage of using a sales process is that the consumer has time to evaluate what he really wants to do. Working a defined process is the smart way to sell. It allows the buyer time to decide if he really wants to complete the transaction. But more important, it provides a way to make a repeat buyer out of him. Books about making our customers raving fans are borne out of this concept. People who are pleased with their decisions and are serviced properly return to do more business.

In today's competitive world, there are too many alternatives for the buyer to consider. We need to give our prospective customers plenty of reasons to buy. By helping them achieve their objectives they will be happy and continue to buy from us. I believe "on purpose" selling is the only way this can be done. "On purpose" selling occurs when we use a process—a process that is compassionate, informative and provides added value.

As you read this book, ask yourself these questions:

> Do you have a repeatable selling process?
> Are you doing things "on purpose" or by accident?
> Can you articulate the sales principles you employ?
> Could you teach these principles to someone else?

If you can answer yes to these questions, then you should probably be writing this book. But if you can't, then I suggest you read this book very carefully. Afterwards, come back and see if you can answer these questions.

I am convinced that when a salesperson can answer these questions, he will have the knowledge necessary to attain the top level of sales success. He will be able to achieve consistent results that will distinguish him from all other sales people. I believe it is virtually impossible for anyone to achieve consistent, outstanding sales results unless he knows the answers to these four questions.

So, as you read this book, write down the principles as you discover them and then commit them to memory. Internalize them if possible. Then test your sales process and see if you are using these principles to build lasting relationships. I guarantee that your sales results will improve dramatically once you employ an "on purpose" selling method.

CHAPTER TWO

The Truth Will Set You Free

Selling is all about relationships. It is about helping people discover what they don't know or understand about a particular product or service. This is a noble calling. It requires integrity, character, patience, persistence, compassion and a true desire to help others. As sales people, we may find ourselves doing things for people and not getting directly paid. There is no rule book for sales. Nobody ever said it would be fair. But there are some very sound and proven principles that we can apply. If we do these principles consistently, then we will attain success. I believe this with the very core of my being.

As I said previously, before I started selling life insurance, I sold a variety of other products, such as shoes, sporting goods, housewares, appliances and electronic equipment. I feel I was successful in all of those endeavors. There was quantitative proof to support my success. I always had the most transactions and highest dollar volume of sales. Why?

Certainly, I was motivated to succeed and excel. I put my full effort into doing and being the best I could be. But I believe I am successful because I help people obtain what they wanted. I learned early on that people know what they want. They just may not know how to get it.

I must admit that when I first began selling insurance, I was fearful. I did not know if I could succeed. Commissions sales is a difficult business and finding your own prospects is a lot different than working in a store and serving people who come to you to buy. The hardest part of selling life insurance is the rejection. Since life insurance is a complex financial product, buyers are reticent and wary. This is *not* a good combination. They tend to ask hard questions and want to know details they don't really understand.

Every time a hard question was asked, I could feel the fear and pain. Now I know that the 'hard questions' have much more to do with my own insecurities and weaknesses than about the product. I had to learn to adjust my own attitude about the buyer's perceptions. Typical questions that caused me anxiety had to do with how the product compared to competitor's products, how the assumptions used in the illustration related to interest rates, whether term insurance was a better buy than permanent products, and other factors which I didn't control.

When these questions came up (and invariably they do), I would often worry about the impact the answer would have on the prospect. I would hesitate before I answered them. That was not because I didn't want to tell the truth, but because I was afraid the truth would cause the prospect to decide against buying. As you know, commission sales is very scary. Rejection can mean the difference between paying your bills and financial desperation. (I have been on the financial edge and I don't ever want to be there again.) Ultimately, I would answer the question and hope that my answer would satisfy the prospect's concerns.

It was this experience that caused me to reassess my attitude towards the sales process. It became a matter of "problem, problem, who's got the problem?" I discovered I was taking too much responsibility for the problems. Instead of feeling confident that I was a messenger and acting on behalf of my prospect/client, I found I was trying to defend the products and accept responsibility for the complexity and problems.

I learned early in my life that telling the truth was always the best policy. Sometimes what we know and what we fear are in conflict. I don't know what you think about the Bible or if you have spiritual preferences, but I personally believe the Bible is the inerrant word of God. That means it is perfect in all respects. As a result of my belief, I accept the Bible's teachings as being the best way to handle a problem. Regardless of how you feel about the Bible, most people would agree there is much wisdom within its pages.

There are two Bible verses that come to mind when I think of my fears. The first is, "the Truth will set you free." To me, that means that if you always deal in truth, then you never have to worry about what you have said to whom. You can live in total confidence that there are no alligators that are about to get you. Second, the Bible says that "perfect love casts out fear." If we treat others with respect and "agape love," then there is nothing to fear. The Bible says that no man can hurt us. So, even if they don't buy from us, there will always be another day. These two verses (among others) have formulated my sales philosophy.

When I finally defined my philosophy, I determined I had three alternatives if I was going to survive in the sales world. One of the main characteristics of success is being able to determine the downside and assess its impact. Successful people always measure the possible loss. Once they determine the downside is not relevant, they can go on.

Selling Alternatives

My first alternative was to stop selling insurance. Second, I could lie when I was confronted with tough issues (although it wasn't much of an option.) Or third, I could change my selling style and try to develop a method that would eliminate the power of the objections. The ability to look at the worst case scenario and use it as a base line for the pricetag of success is an important tool.

Let's look at each of these alternatives and see why I elected to change my method.

I could stop selling the product. Every salesman at one time or another has thought about quitting. For me, what has made me continue is that I like selling so much. But if you don't believe in your product and what your product can do for your customer, then you have to question whether you should continue. So let's look closely at the professionalism of our product.

7

At one time or another we have all questioned our sanity and the wisdom of choosing a sales career. I already told you I thought my mother was going to die when she heard I was going to sell insurance. Here she had supported me through four years of college and then I had gone on to graduate school. She wanted an attorney, a banker, a corporate president, not an insurance salesman. Most readers will readily say, every career has some element of sales to it. Somehow being a professional salesman was not her vision for me.

When you evaluate a product, ask yourself whether you can be a professional selling your products. Do they meet these four basic requirements?

1. Is it competitive?
2. Will people buy it?
3. Can you competently explain it?
4. Can you deliver what you promise?

Is your product competitive? There is no way to really know if your product is competitive unless you survey your competition. Who markets a product similar to yours? What are the differences and similarities? Can you create a logical and honest analysis that demonstrates the strengths and weaknesses of your product contrasted to the others?

There is nothing more humbling than to find yourself disadvantaged because someone knows his product better than you do. Trying to sell in a closed market presents unlimited problems. Who needs it? You must know your competition. You have to understand what the consumer will be seeing when you leave. Unless you are able to build a protective barrier around your product and services, you will be susceptible to the competitive pressures.

Once you analyze your product and determine you have a great story to tell, you will have confidence in your product and can aggressively pursue your market. Without that confidence, you will hold back your best effort. Most consumers want the best product they can buy for the money. They need to have a logical understanding of why your product is superior. Unless you can show them clearly and concisely the advantages of your product, you are open to competitive attack. The best strategy is to become the competition. Know the other products so well that you actually sell against yourself. You become the buyer for the client and demonstrate the pros and cons of every viable alternative he might consider.

If you have earned the trust and confidence of your buyer, then you will prevail. If you haven't earned it, then you can expect he will not do business with you.

Will people buy it? This may seem like an obvious question, but have you assessed the demand for the product you are selling. What is the market for this product or service? How many people already have it? The answer dictates the sales strategy.

A new product will cause you to create demand. You have to demonstrate why your product does the job better than what people are using today. This means you have to fully understand the alternative solutions that are commonly being used. You then have to assess the cost and the advantages of changing. What is the learning curve for being able to use this new product? What are the costs of switching? What impact does it have on other systems? What are the political considerations in implementing the change? Unless you ask all of the questions and find out all of the pluses and minuses, you are wasting your time.

Asking these questions may seem redundant. But always ask yourself this question, "Would you buy the product knowing what you know?" If you assess your selling logic from the perspective of the buyer, you can usually anticipate the reasons why he might not want to do it.

If your product is not new to the market, the problems you face change a little. You still have to assess the cost of change. But the current status was chosen for some basic reasons. What are the reasons? Who made the decision? What were the factors that went into the decision? Are any of those factors different? Knowing those factors, would you make the same decision today? Would the customer?

People do not like change. Habits are hard to break. The willingness to change is usually tied to one of three reasons—lower cost, more efficient utilization of resources, or politics—they like you and want to do business with you. But even so, all things must be at least equal. In order to determine which reason works, you have to know all of the facts. We will look at fact gathering in another chapter. But remember, selling in a vacuum is foolish. Get all of the information you can *before* you make a recommendation.

Can you competently explain it? Some products are so technical that they require a Ph.D. to explain them. You must feel competent to market your product. Customers know when you are insecure and feel like you don't know what you are talking about. Unfortunately, this is a Catch 22. When you first start, you can not possibly know everything there is to know about a product. However, if you wait until you are an expert, you may be bankrupt.

Using other people's experience is a fast track to knowledge. Not only do you benefit financially from their expertise, but you also have on the job training. You can learn while you earn. Most beginners are so greedy to keep what they haven't earned, that they can't envision bringing someone else along. It is an affront to their esteem. This is pure foolishness. The only problem is between the ears. Pride is the source of much failure. So you have a choice; if you want to learn, but you can't afford to starve, consider a sidekick, mentor or partner—not as a permanent arrangement, but just until you get the hang of things. Then you can venture off on your own.

Your customer deserves the best. If you are offering only half of the pie to your customer—the product but not the full service—then you are shortchanging both the customer and yourself. The customer is shortchanged because he is only getting part of what he thought he was buying (unmet and unspoken expectations). You are shortchanged because you have lengthened your learning time and perhaps jeopardized your long-term relationship with the customer.

Can you deliver what you promise? Obviously, this is related to the previous issue, but it goes deeper. You might have the best product in the world, but your company cannot deliver what it promised. The manufacturing process is too slow, the raw material isn't available, all of the bugs have not been worked out yet. There are ever so many issues, some unforeseeable. But you need to assess the obvious ones. If you are making promises that cannot be fulfilled, you need to know it. You need to realize it right now.

Too often, in our exuberance and enthusiasm, we ascribe attributes to our products that may not exist yet because the ideas are still on the drawing board and the concepts have not been truly tested or proven. I will demonstrate later how this type of selling causes the prospect/customer to lose confidence in you and the product or service. We salespeople need to be careful to not overstate the benefits or the services that the client can expect. It is better to always underpromise and overdeliver.

I could lie! What if the answers to your sales questions are "no"? You could lie. Not me, you say. I never would. But before you go on, think about the temptation every salesperson experiences as he goes about his daily tasks. You've seen it. I think very few people will deliberately set out to lie and defraud the customer. But circumstances often dictate the temptation. The ability to avoid this temptation is directly related to our personal security and financial well-being.

Is it lying when the salesman promises something that can't happen the way he promised it? The company announces it can deliver the product/service/software on a specific schedule only to discover that due to technical difficulties (circumstances beyond the company's control), the company has to change the schedule. Where does that leave you, the salesperson? Was your representation a lie or was it circumstantial? Did the company lie to you because they knew they were having problems and were pressured into a premature announcement? Warranties are written to protect customers from "lies." If the product is fully guaranteed and can deliver what is promised 100% of the time, warranties would not be needed.

Service agreements are the result of products that do not meet the customer's expectations. It's almost like saying, "We know you are going to have problems. We stand behind our product and we will fix those problems." Yet as salespeople, we represented this

wonderful product that would do all of these wonderful things. We
never really acknowledged the servicing and technical support problems the client would face.

Look at the disclaimers on the labels of most products or the
SEC-required prospectus that accompanies most financial products. Those disclaimers would not be needed if the products really
could deliver what was represented by you, the salesperson. These
discrepancies create an environment that can cause salespeople
much anxiety. These gray areas create the ethical issues we must
all face and resolve for ourselves.

It is the gray areas that cause the customer to ask the hard
questions in the interview. As the buyer becomes more sophisticated, the more sophisticated the questions will be. The buyer really wants to know. In order to overcome these hard questions we
basically have two choices. We can shine them on by passing over
the hard questions and down playing the questions as unimportant.
Or, we can choose to face the questions directly and educate the
consumer about their concerns. By demonstrating to them the im-
plications of the risks, we demonstrate that we are to be trusted.
Remember, people do what they want to do when they want to do
it anyway!

If the customer is uncomfortable with you and your explanation, he is likely to pass on the deal and go on with his life. If you
have invested many hours only to have the customer move on, the
cost is high. Your sales effort to hold on gives rise to the perception
that sales is high pressure. The buyer/seller tension can cause much
anxiety and misunderstanding. On the other hand, if you play it
totally straight, you might lose this deal, but you will retain the
right to come back with another idea.

Ask yourself, what are you really selling—products or relationships.

I could develop a riskless sales method. The tension between
the buyer and seller is what led me to develop the "riskless" selling
method. I firmly believe it is possible to build a sales process that
is so respectable, ethical and honest, that you can proudly approach
anybody who might be a prospect for your services or product.

You can do so with the knowledge that you have something valuable to say and offer. More importantly, you also know that if your reputation precedes you, it will be in a positive way.

The secret is to fully understand the natural anxiety your customer/prospect feels and anticipate his anxiety before you engage in the sales process. If you can fully assess the reasonable issues and problems that you are likely to face with virtually every prospective buyer, you can then build a delivery system of information that substantially reduces the likelihood the buyer will not buy from you.

You must remember what you are selling. You sell *relationships*. You sell the right to continue a dialogue with this prospective buyer. If you ever lose that right, the relationship is over and you have to find someone else. Good prospects are hard to find. Building a relationship is even harder. We will look at this more thoroughly in a later chapter, but I want to highlight the process for you now.

The first step in the riskless sales process is to carefully assess the prospect's need for your product or service. You need to be able to sift through the universe of prospective buyers and ascertain whether or not the person you want to approach really needs what you have to offer. Marketing and attracting qualified buyers is another area which is beyond the scope of this book. But once you identify a prospect, what is your strategy? What do you say to the prospect to instill his confidence in you? What are you selling in the first interview?

Once you identify your prospect and establish your credibility, you must accurately and quickly communicate what you have to offer and why. In your opinion, you have the unique ability to help him. This must be done in a non-threatening way which allows the prospect to decide if he agrees with your assessment. Does he, in fact have a need for your product or service? Is he willing to consider an alternative? Does he believe you can provide him with a path for evaluation? You are asking him to invest in you. Can you deliver? At this stage of the process, the secret to success is for the prospective customer to be able to differentiate between agreeing to buy your product and agreeing to look carefully at the advantages you have to offer.

If you both agree the customer should look fur-ther, then you must accurately gather as much information as you can from him. This fact finding must be systematic and complete. In order to accurately determine whether you can help him, you must know what he knows. You have to climb into the customer's skin and think like he thinks. More importantly, you must determine whether or not you can help him. This may seem obvious, but the sale is made here. If you do the right job of gathering data, you actually assure the success of your process.

Once you gather the facts, you then have to for-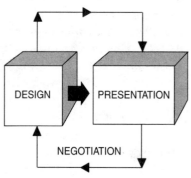mulate a plan design that will accurately reflect the prospect's current situation. Is it as simple as the car he wants to purchase or the type of shoes he wants, or is it a complex recounting of his current financial situation? Remember, he will tell you what he wants to do. You have to develop good listening skills and use these skills to understand the prospect's needs. Once you totally understand his current position, you can then reflect on possible alternatives and present your ideas.

The design/presentation function is really a negotiation of sorts. You are relating to the prospect your understanding of his needs and he responds by affirming or denying your understanding. This becomes an interactive process until he feels you understand his needs and have accurately represented his alternatives. As you hone in on the prospect's needs and give him viable alternatives to solve those needs, you begin to move towards a decision. This interactive process will probably take several attempts before the prospect finally agrees that the solutions fit his needs.

But in the problem-solving environment, the interactive process is the sale. It is during this back and forth process that the client talks himself into taking action. If you are unable to find a common ground, the negotiation stops.

Implementation occurs only when the prospect agrees that the solutions you have presented meet his needs and he is willing to move forward on your recommendations. This is commonly called the close.

So, which method of selling will you use? Life is a series of choices. All of the marketing data on consumer preferences show that buyers want choices. This means the sales professionals have to change their approach. It means that you have to shift from solution selling to problem selling.

This paradigm shift (changing the way you think about things to a new way of thinking) will cause each professional salesperson to assess the method of sales he currently employs.

Larry Wilson wrote about partnering in the 90's. He said we have to come around to the other side of the table and start thinking and acting like the partner of the buyer. He is dead right! Studies on consumer preferences show that consumers want advisors. As these consumers convert their needs into buying decisions, they will seek vendors who will sell to them the way they want to be sold. Professional salespeople need to become sellers who appeal to those preferences.

CHAPTER THREE

The Magic Box

Once upon a time, there was a magic box. It was called a magic box because of its unusual capabilities. It could produce unlimited amounts of money from blank pieces of paper. That's right, money from blank paper. All you had to do was place a blank piece of paper into the slot on the side of the box and out came a large denomination bill—a $100, $500 or $1000 bill from

the slot at the bottom. Imagine if you had a magic box like that. What do you think you would do?

Realizing this is not a trick question, most everyone tells me that they would put as many pieces of blank paper into the box as fast as they could. Wouldn't you run around and find all the paper you could and then shove it into the box? Well, wouldn't you?

Would you really care how this box worked? Would you care what this box was made of? I doubt it. You would be very careful to protect your box and take very good care of it. I doubt if you

16

would need to know every detail about how the box worked. All you would want to do is make sure you had enough paper available to put into the box.

After a while, you begin to notice you have a major problem. Your box jams periodically—sometimes for days. Using your best problem-solving skills, you decide that maybe you are putting the paper in a little too fast. So you decide you will modulate the flow and slow down when you put the paper into the box. Lo and behold, this works ... at least for a while. Your box starts up again and produces money, just the way it always did.

Sometime later, you begin to notice that your box jams and won't produce anything for hours, sometimes days. In fact, there are times when it could take weeks or maybe months before the box will unjam and start producing money again. You check your paper flow and discover that it's okay, the flow is perfect—just the way you planned it. So, that only leaves one other variable. It must be the paper itself. You begin to do a quality test and discover that the box actually rejects certain bonds and grades of paper.

Now, if this were the case, what would you do to protect your box?

Most people say that they would determine which type of paper the box liked. In order to do this, you would have to develop some type of filter—a filter that would differentiate between good paper and bad paper. You would have to make certain your box only received the best grade of paper. Realizing this, you develop a way to test each piece of paper and, to your amazement, the box begins to produce again, just like it once did.

Fortunately, this story does have a happy ending. The magic box works forever and never stops again. Now, wouldn't you like to own a magic box just like this one?

Unfortunately, none of us will probably ever own this type of magic box, unless we are counterfeiters. But you have something that is equally as valuable: your sales organization. That's correct. Your sales organization is just like this magic box and it will only stop working when you do. Your organization is an integral part of the sales process.

In my insurance business, my organization (my magic box) does all of the repeatable work. This repeatable work is the work which can be systematized and performed by either a computer or a non-professional. My organization consists of administration, design, and production components. The actual sales aspect, finding the prospects, is done by me. I am the one who inserts the paper into the magic box and the organization processes the paper into dollar bills.

To extend the analogy, the flow and grade of the prospects can impact the productivity of your organization. In the insurance business, we call bad prospects 'china eggs.' They won't hatch but they look pretty and draw a lot of attention. As you put more and more of these kinds of prospects into your organization, the box will either jam because the work flow is too fast or because the prospects take too much time and never buy. Discerning a good prospect from a bad prospect is an important part of keeping your magic box from jamming.

Ask yourself this question. How many salespeople, who are properly trained and experienced, would lack the confidence they need to make a sale if they had enough good prospects? None?? That's what I think. Virtually every salesperson has confidence that he or she can make a sale eventually, if there are enough good prospects. I remember thinking very early in my career that if I could just line up the good prospects outside my office, I could make an unlimited amount of sales. The rhetorical question was, "How do I line them up?"

It was this question that started me thinking about the sales process and the magic box. As long as you put good prospects into your system, you will make sales. Whether you are a lone ranger, an independent with no staff, or you have a business organization backing you up, the most effective sales process will always be the same.

Let me give you an illustration. A good friend of mine, Jim Pittman, lives in Portland, Oregon. He is a very successful life insurance salesman. He tells the story of his friend who was a very successful crew member on a racing yacht. The yacht would always come in third or fourth place. The crew knew all of the routines and had learned all of the skills. But no matter how much they wanted to win, they could only come in third or fourth.

One day, this fellow's big break came. He was asked to crew with the best team. He naturally jumped at the opportunity. Months went by and the team continued it's winning ways. The friend was integrated into the team and the team just kept getting better—improving a little with each new race.

Jim asked his friend what the difference was. "On the first team you always came in third or fourth," Jim began, "but now you come in first. Can you quantify the difference?"

"Sure," the friend said. "We just do things a little bit better." They tied the knots a little faster, ran up the jib a little quicker, made the turns a little cleaner. Everything was just 10% better. The moral is to practice and practice until you get it just right.

That story made me ask myself, is there a way to do things just a little bit better? Is there any one of us who really believes that the top sales people are just luckier than the rest? I don't think so. There are selling skills that make a difference—knowing the products, understanding the applications, knowing the competition, understanding your customer. If you can just do these things a little better, you can improve the results.

But what skills are there to practice? What can you as a salesperson do a little bit better so you can get the results you dream about? Hopefully, you will know what to practice when you finish reading this book. The very idea of practicing is at the heart of improving. But practice does not make perfect. It is *perfect* practice that makes perfect. You need to learn what to practice.

I am reminded of my youth. I loved baseball. I would go anywhere and do anything to play. I was not an outstanding player, but I could hold my own with most of the guys. Every night, I practiced fielding ground balls. For hours I would throw the ball against the wall and practice catching it. I would practice throwing against another wall. I would practice my form and pitch until I was tired. Unfortunately, I could not practice batting. So I would throw the ball up in the air and then hit it against the wall. The point is, I always had my glove on my hand and a ball in my mitt.

Years later, when I started to teach baseball, I realized that I had not learned the principles of baseball. I had learned how to play and I had practiced, but I had not practiced the right things. There were actual skills I should have learned and practiced, but was never taught. As I finally learned these skills, I taught them. I taught people how to field, how to slide, how to hold a bat, etc. I taught people to practice the skills they needed to learn to play a better game.

Selling is an art. It requires an excellent understanding of people and why they buy. This knowledge, combined with the right product knowledge and professional services, can bring sales success to anyone. But unless you apply this knowledge and practice it, you are like the formula one race car team with no driver. You have to match the practice with the skills.

Let's look more closely at these foundational skills.

CHAPTER FOUR

Do We Sell Problems Or Solutions?

As I mentioned in the last chapter, the foundational sales skill is understanding people. Salespeople need to be people engineers so they can deal effectively with their many facets and their many differences. Not everyone will agree with you or think like you. That's why you have to adapt your communication style to appeal to as wide of a range of buyers as possible. This needs to be done ethically and congruently. You can't be something you are not.

Most people operate from two dynamic positions. They have fears and needs. This is the common bond that exists between most of us. I say most of us, because I don't think very many salespeople are exempt from these same factors. At our very core as humans there are needs that must be met (food, safety, shelter, emotional stability) and there is often the fear that these needs will not be met. Maslow's hierarchy of needs spoke directly of these issues. A person can begin to focus on others only when he has set aside his own fears.

When I speak, I will often do a survey of my audience and ask them this question, "Do we sell *problems* or do we sell *solutions*?" I ask for a show of hands of those who believe we sell problems, and a show of hands of those who believe we sell solutions. If I asked you that question, what would you answer? If you answered solutions, then you fall exactly in line with 99% of the audience response I typically receive. Imagine that! Virtually 99% of every sales audience says *we sell solutions*. That's a pretty unanimous vote. But is that what we actually sell?

Let's examine this question for a minute. Do you believe that sales is, by definition, adversarial? It can be. I have found the entire process of overcoming buyer reticence/reluctance very adversarial. You, as a sales professional are attempting to convince the prospective buyer that he should be doing something that he isn't particularly interested in doing. After all, there must be some reason why he hasn't taken action yet. If you see our job as overcoming this inertia, then you are truly selling solutions.

The buyer has something you want—his money! You are offering something he doesn't necessarily want—your products and/ or services. And even if the buyer does want it, he probably wants to pay less for it than you are asking.

Assuming you have not created too much anxiety for the prospective buyer, you might say that the problem and the solution are in equilibrium with the cost. As long as the buyer is not focused on the cost, he usually remains calm and peaceful. However, once the cost is divulged to the prospective buyer, his anxiety heightens and the "sales war" begins.

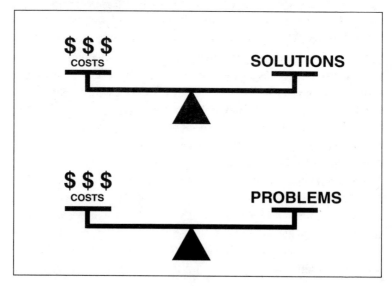

DO WE SELL PROBLEMS OR SOLUTIONS?

As the conflict intensifies, the cost for the solution grows heavier. In other words, as you try to convince your prospective buyer that the solution is worth the cost, the buyer focuses more and more on cost. Most sales trainers tell you at that point to stress the benefits more. In other words, load up the solutions side of the scale with additional reasons why this purchase makes sense. But there is only one way the benefits make any sense, and that's if the *problem* is clearly understood. That's the proper time to stress the benefits—when the buyer is *looking for the solution.*

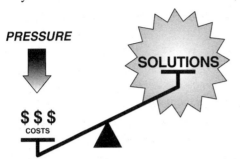

Our sales instincts suggest that when the buyers fully understand the benefits and value of our solution, they will readily agree to purchase our recommendation. For me, this thinking is wrong. It is a sales strategy laden with conflict and tension for both the buyer and the seller. I win when the buyer buys. I lose when the buyer escapes. Of course, we have convinced ourselves that when the buyer buys, he wins. But ask yourself, does he feel like he won? How do you think they feel when it is all over?

The more we focus on the solutions, the more the buyer is going to focus on the costs. We have to change his paradigm and get him to focus on the real issue—*his unsolved problems.*

When the problem is clearly understood, the buyer will want to solve it. Is there anything you really have to have, that you have not already purchased? We must remember that people

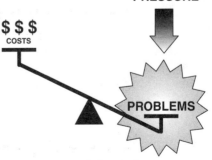

will always do what they want to do. Our job is to make the problem big enough for the buyer to feel the pain of the problem, not the solution. In fact, we have to help the buyer understand the magnitude of the problem. But it can only be accomplished when he participates in the discovery process. When the problem is so big that the buyer is willing to pay any reasonable price to make the problem go away, we have a sale.

This has often been referred to as *needs* selling. However, there is a difference between perceived needs and real needs. If the buyer doesn't think he needs whatever we are selling, then he isn't likely to buy it. Once the buyer understands he has a problem and is left on his own to figure out the best way to solve the problem, we have a viable prospect. I believe it is our job to take the buyer through this curve of understanding.

There is a specific reasoning process every buyer goes through as he processes his problem and then ultimately makes a buying decision. If we can tap into that reasoning process and participate in his understanding of the relationship between the "pain and the gain" (doing nothing and doing something), we are then positioned to implement the decision after he agrees to take action. We'll study this sales process in depth in the next chapter.

But first, let me again ask you that all-important question. What is it you sell? Problems or solutions?

Remember, 99% of the audiences say we sell solutions. I would like you to consider the premise that we really sell problems, not needs, not solutions, but problems. The better we are at defining and communicating the real problems to our prospects and buyers, the better we will be at helping them implement the proper solutions. Remember, we sell problems and we implement solutions.

Somehow the whole concept of selling came to suggest that we have a mystical ability and capacity to make someone do something he doesn't really want to do. But let me ask you another question. When was the last time anybody made you do something you didn't want to do? How did it feel? Were you happy about it? Did you feel good afterward? Probably not! In fact, you may have been a little bit angry about it.

In the insurance business, when someone purchases an insurance product he doesn't really want, we call it buyer's remorse. But more frequently it is called a *lapse*. Most incidents of buyer's remorse translates into a returned product or an unhappy customer. If this happens, we have wasted both our time and our energy.

The idea that we can manipulate, cajole, or pressure someone into doing anything he doesn't want to do is an old-fashioned selling idea. It is a total myth. Today, consumers are too smart to allow themselves to be sold. There is too much information available and competition in the marketplace is too keen for them to tolerate behaviors that make them uncomfortable. Buyers have learned to beware. They want to control their "buy." The job of the professional salesperson is to facilitate the sale, not high pressure a decision. Remember, we *sell* the problems, and *implement* the solutions. We must become known for the problems we solve, *not* the solutions we sell.

Let's go back now, to the magic box and the concept of a filter.

CHAPTER FIVE

The Selling Process

As you know by now, the magic box is merely a conceptual description of our selling process and a repeatable sales process is the heart of our sales success. Why? We need repeatable systems so we can take the guesswork out of selling. Secondly, we need visual stories that can bring the more complex concepts into sharp focus. It is a real skill to be able to take abstract ideas and make them visual and understandable.

The magic box offers a unique way for us to think about our own organizations. In order to be successful, we all need to think like business owners. If we think like employees, we act like employees. Employees do not take risks and are unable to visualize success the way a business owner can.

The magic box provides an organized way to think about our selling process. The sales process is a specific set of repeatable steps that leads to the sale. The process is a path for increasing our sales results by steadfastly applying proven communication principles and learning to use them effectively. The ultimate key to increased productivity is having systems and delegating non-productive tasks.

As a result, our magic box provides a conceptual way to analyze our productivity. If we can formulate ways to be more productive, to spend less time doing unproductive tasks, we can either get better results in the same time frame or the same results in less time. Either way we become more efficient and effective. Think about how many tasks you can put into your magic box.

If you remember, the two main reasons the magic box stopped producing were either because the flow of paper bogged down the box's productivity or the wrong grade of paper was being shoved into the box and could not be processed efficiently. In our business, we need to modulate our flow of paper (prospects and clients) and select the right grade of paper (our valuable prospects for future sales). It is too easy to pick the wrong paper if you do not have a standard. You must protect your organization from inefficient prospects and ineffective work flow.

I call this protection mechanism a *filter*. If your water wasn't safe to drink, you would filter out the impurities to provide clean drinking water. Filters are used in many functional aspects of our life to make certain the impurities are removed. A prospecting filter separates out the good prospects from the bad ones. If you spend your productive time seeing productive prospects, your sales results will increase. If your sales results don't increase, then there is either something wrong with your products or your sales story.

Top salespeople use a filter to distinguish between profitable and unprofitable activity and/or prospects. According to the studies I have done with top salespeople, their filter is the most valuable selling tool they own. Why? First, it heads them in the right direction. It keeps them on target. Without it, we would all meander aimlessly, often toward the wrong objective. Second, a good filter prevents them from misusing their resources and helps them determine the best way to spend their valuable time. After all, time is really our most precious asset.

Do you have a clear picture of your ideal prospect? Do you have that picture in writing and do you look at it frequently? It is not good enough to just say, "anyone who will buy." Our studies show that the best salespeople all *prequalify* their buyers. These high performers only deal with people who are *prequalified* to buy. That's right. They virtually make the sale before the sale. They effectively eliminate the unprofitable buyers from the queue.

What does this mean? It means your filter has to be very discreet. The prospect must pass a *test* before you will do business with him. That is a critical difference. Instead of finding people who will do business with you, think about finding people you want to do business with. The prospect must meet a certain criteria that you pre-establish and acknowledge before you even meet him. What type of factors go into this prequalification criteria?

Well, your test design should depend significantly on the product you are selling. In the financial world, the beginning criteria is usually age, income, net worth, occupation and family situation. But to prequalify them, I think the filter needs to be much more discerning.

If I am selling to a business owner, I want him to be successful, have employees and have a desire to see the business continue. Hopefully, there is at least one family member involved in the business. I want my prospective company/client to be profitable and have value worth protecting. If there are no family members, then I want the partners to have a desire to see the business continue after they retire. Remember, we sell problems. If they have no problems, they do not need us.

If I am dealing with an estate planning situation, the prospect needs to have an estate greater than $3,000,000 or at least one that will ultimately grow to this size or larger. My prospects should have an adequate income, plus some assets that I consider heirlooms (which means they want to keep them in the family forever). They must love someone or something so much that they are willing to do the right thing to protect their assets for the benefit of their family.

Other products and services may have different criteria. If I were selling shoes, I would want someone with feet. Just kidding! But the customer must need shoes or why would they be shopping? Can they afford good shoes? Cheap shoes? Dress shoes? Loafers? Are they able to make a decision?

If I were selling automobiles, the customer would need to have good credit before I would waste time on him. Perhaps he has bought this brand of automobile before. He may be looking to upgrade to a new year and model so I would ask whether he has a good trade-in, among other questions.

Each sales professional knows the best criteria for identifying or categorizing a good, qualified buyer. They can think back on their best sales and see a pattern of success. Why not try to repeat that pattern? Look for people who fit the pattern.

This does not mean you can't deal with people outside your criteria. But why? Have a reason and don't just accept any prospect because "you have nothing better to do." Top sellers all do the right things right. They are unwilling to waste time on unproductive efforts.

Frankly, in the beginning of my career, I wasted too much time. Certainly not on purpose, but because I was afraid of not seeing people. I spent too much time chasing buyers who were not specific to my defined market. I would crawl over a field of barbed wire, land mines, rusty nails and broken glass to make a sale. I would drive 60 miles south in the morning, 120 miles north for an afternoon appointment and then return to my local area for an evening appointment. While I only talked to people who were interested in buying from me, I would go anywhere to find them.

After the second year, I primarily worked with referrals. But I did a good job of prequalifying them on the phone by asking them questions and establishing a rapport with them before I would go out to see them. My manager, Ralph Brown told me "Guy, you only do business with people who are predisposed to buy." Now I was prequalifying them, but they still didn't always meet my ideal profile. I was dealing with unqualified buyers. Little did I know that I had stumbled onto one of the most important keys to successful selling. Remember, a prequalifying a buyer is a major element to increased productivity.

An Unqualified Buyer

I have continued to use this term "unqualified buyer." What do I mean by an unqualified buyer? An unqualified buyer is a prospect that does not fit the profile I developed to determine my ideal market. If a prospect does not fit this profile, then I should not spend time doing business with him. The prospect profile I developed was based on the goal I had set for my business. I knew that other agents were selling millions of dollars of insurance to upscale clients. I proposed to participate in that market but I would not be able to reach that goal if I limited my activity to buyers who did not meet the demographics of this type of client. I had to refrain from going after buyers who were not part of my long-term business strategy. This was very hard to do, especially since I had established work habits that were based on a high level of activity.

Let me make this more clear. In the early stages of any career, the most important aspect of success is activity. Practice, practice, practice. But there comes a time when we need to upgrade our prospects in order to improve our productivity. In other words, "how many heads of hair can a barber cut?" You can be the best barber in the world, but if you can only do four haircuts an hour, you are limited in how much money you can make. There are only two solutions, delegate (hire more barbers) or charge more money per hair cut. Both have limitations.

As insurance agents, productivity is increased by seeing more of the right type of people and selling a high percentage of them. But before you can do this, most agents have to earn the right. They have to develop a clientele, a following and then upgrade who they talk to.

If I want to solve estate tax and business succession problems, then I needed to have prospects who have those problems. That's simple enough to understand. It's like the old Willie Sutton story. They asked him why he robbed banks and he said, "That's where the money is."

Most of the prospects I was calling on back then were not banks. They would never own their own businesses and probably would not accumulate large estates. They were wonderful people and I love them and their families. I appreciate their friendship and willingness to do business with me, especially when I was first starting to sell. I was and am totally dedicated to helping them. But would they qualify for my long-term target market now?

During those early years, I financially survived on the income I derived from my "nonprofile" customers, as I systematically tried to upgrade my market. The question I have to ask myself is, would I have developed my market faster if I had exclusively worked on my target profile? I don't know the answer to that question. I do know that I had to survive and I had to pay the staff I was training and developing. I made the best decisions I could at the time. But I look back now and can clearly see I wasted time on unprofitable sales while I avoided going after my primary market.

I did not have the courage to redirect my activity so I could go after the type of cases I wanted to deal with and am dealing with today. Was that inexperience? Was that due to a lack of knowledge and confidence? Was that the lack of primary business contacts? Was that my own inability to prospect in those markets? Was I afraid?

The answers to those questions are unimportant to me today because I eventually solved the problem. If I had to do it again, I would have concentrated more time developing professional contacts. Ask yourself, what are you doing to penetrate the market of your choice? Do you have a defined market? Can you improve faster if you spend more time going after the type of clients you want to develop?

Your Selling System

This question is a personal one that only you can answer for yourself. But I do know that each of us has to combine the right prospecting skills with the right selling system. Unless you have a solid, tested, repeatable selling system, it is impossible for you to have long term success with the upscale customers. Let's look at the general makeup of a selling system.

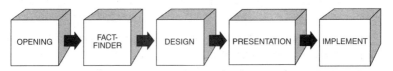

There should be nothing new in this diagram. The simplicity of the selling system is based upon logic. We all know the basic steps. First you must open the case, then do a factfinder. Once you have the facts, you must design your recommendations, present them and then, hopefully, implement the recommendation. Although this may sound insanely simple, you will see there is much sophistication (referred to as *competent consciousness*) that goes into this process. The learning process can be referred to as learning curves.

There are four phases of learning that most people go through. In the beginning, you start with a foreboding. This is referred to as *unconscious incompetence*. You don't know what you don't know. Then you begin to get a sense of what lies ahead and your sense of foreboding turns into stark fear. This is called *conscious incompetence*. You begin to know what you don't know.

The third step is gaining the upper hand and starting to do things "on purpose." This is called *conscious competence*. You know what you know and you know what you don't know. Finally, you become a real pro and everything comes second nature to you. You are now an *unconscious competent*. You have forgotten more than most people will ever know.

Why is a selling process necessary? After all, some people are so influential and charismatic, they can just walk in and tell someone what they should do. And, you know what? The client actually does it. I don't think I could build my career on this approach. I need a process so I can minimize my errors and the chance of failure.

The reason most people fail in sales is because after they make it into a war, somebody wins and somebody loses. If the prospect offers up one or more objections that the sales person cannot overcome, the prospect wins the adversarial confrontation.

The sales process is all about converting this adversarial process into a win/win situation. Selling is not about selling. The sale is the ultimate outcome and how we get paid. But selling is about helping people achieve what they want. Remember, people do what they want to do when they want to do it. So, why not help them do what they want to do and get credit for helping them?

The Four Basic Objections

A prospect senses if you are just trying to sell him and if you are really not prepared. He knows if you are green and do not trust your ability to really help him. Most buyers typically won't buy if they feel uncertain or worried. These feelings can cause the prospective buyer to offer up one or more of the four primary objections: *no need, no hurry, no money or no confidence.* If you have done the right job of filtering your clients and you have successfully worked your sales process, then I have found you will automatically eliminate at least three of these four objections. We'll look more fully at these objections in a future chapter that specifically deals with. So, let's get back to our filter.

I mentioned the importance of a "prequalification filter." There are actually two filters you will want to develop to successfully work this sales system. The first filter eliminates inefficient prospects from going into your magic box—your sales system. But even the most sophisticated computers have a *backup system.* This second filter **is** your backup system—the most important segment in your selling system. I call this the refining process. This filter validates and then verifies the decision your first filter made.

Without this second filter, you run the risk of over-estimating the value of your prospect. With it, you verify the information you have gathered and you develop the foundation for the third step of the sales process, the factfinder. There are two things to keep in mind while you work your selling process at this point. First, the only goal of the opening, is to get to the next step in the process, the factfinder. Second, and most important, the factfinder is where you make the sale, regardless of what product you are selling. A good factfinder will be the ultimate reason the customer buys.

Right now, let's look at the first stage of the selling process— the opening. Practice does not make perfect. If you practice the wrong things, then you will do the wrong things. It is *perfect practice* that makes perfect. Let's learn how we can establish an opening interview that you can practice.

CHAPTER SIX

Developing A Filter

The way to protect your selling process—the magic box—is to make certain that you put the right prospects into your system. The only way to assure this protection is to have a reliable filter.

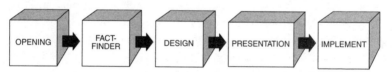

Before we can look at opening the interview, let's review the role of this filter. Where does this filter fit into the process? Why is it important to have this filter? In the last chapter I wrote about prequalifying your prospects. The "opening" filter helps you to determine if your suspect should become a prospect before you waste any time.

The filter is used to *protect* your magic box. Now that may sound strange. Why would you have to protect your selling system? But remember, if you let just any prospect into your system, you run the risk of bogging down the entire process. You have to be discerning. You must have a profile of the customers you want to develop. You need a business plan and a marketing plan so you know where you are going. Remember, do everything "on purpose."

DEVELOPING A FILTER

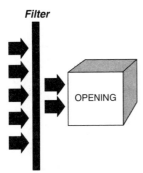

Filter

OPENING

In the beginning of developing your system you may discover that it is hard to turn away from a potential prospect. But as time goes by and you develop your "on purpose" thought process of protecting your selling system, it will be easier to determine who is and who is not a good prospect. The key is having effective criteria. Bruce Etherington has a criteria that I think we all could adopt. He asks himself these four basic questions and poses them to his referral sources.

Among the people you know, who do you know that:
1. Is affluent?
2. Has integrity and character?
3. Can make a decision?
4. Is going places in their career?

If you can "load up your wagon," so to speak, with prospects that fit this criteria, you will rarely make a prospecting mistake. However, in addition to those four questions, I think you should ask about the referral's circumstances. Do they own a business? How many employees do they have? Is it family-held? What type of clients are you looking for in the first place? Just ones who will buy? Do you want to specialize in the estate planning market, or the retirement/investment market? Maybe you want to be known as a specialist in the business succession field.

If you sell hard goods or services, what type of questions should you be asking? Is the basic nature of the questions really any different? Obviously, your prospects must have the ability to pay for any services or products you are selling. You need to have access. You need to know if they use certain kinds of equipment or service processes. You need to find out if they make the decisions or need to consult with others. Is it a committee or a supervisor above them? Are they influential and able to help you build your business with introductions? You see, the same type of questions apply here as well.

This filtering process is always the same. It never changes. Whether you are selling widgets, consulting services or financial products, the process of finding people who are "predisposed to buying" is the same. Unfortunately, very few people take the time to assess the qualities of their buyer. As agents we are so busy trying to be successful (or dealing with our call reluctance) that it is easy to forget the true basics of success. Before anything happens, you have to find somebody to talk to about their problems. But before you can make any money, somebody has to buy something from you. You only have a limited number of hours in a day to accomplish this task. Where is the most productive place to put your time?

So the first filter is your criteria. You have to match each and every name up against this criteria. Here are some general categories you might consider when you build your filter.

1. Occupation
   Industry
   Job title
   Trade Organization

2. Income

3. Net Worth

4. Family situation

5. Affinity groups
   College
   Trade Association
   Community activities
   Service Clubs
   Hobbies
   Charities
   Country Club

6. Peer group

7. Professional Advisors

DEVELOPING A FILTER

The point here is to find ways to network your contacts within your market. Look for ways to provide added value to each of your prospects. The more you can do for them, the more likely they will remember you when there is an opportunity.

I heard of a concept once that seems to fit here. It is called the "shelf of your mind." Think of how you relate to ideas or products and how you remember things. Usually the first thing that pops into your mind is what you respond to. Think of the detergent that comes to mind first. Think of another and another. Eventually it will take several minutes to come up with another. The same is true with automobile advertising, hair spray, deodorants, etc. There are immediate services or products that come to mind when you are expected to recall an item. These are on the "shelf of your mind."

As a marketer of services and product, you want to be so well-positioned with your clients that when your name is mentioned, they immediately associate you with the service or product. That is the difference between prospecting and marketing. Prospecting is an active process of identifying a potential buyer, and if not a buyer, then at least someone who would consider talking to you about the goods and services you offer.

Successful marketing occurs when you are on your client's "shelf." You have succeeded when you are front and center and he thinks of you every time the products and services you represent are mentioned. What can you do to position yourself on the "shelf" of your client's mind?

A filter allows you to sort through the names of people who will talk to you and isolate only the ones you *prequalify* and *want* to talk to about your services and products. What a nice situation to be in, to have a list of prequalified prospects who know what you do, who want to talk to you, and who are accessible because of your marketing skills.

It can be done. But it takes discipline and courage to build a filter that will eventually provide you with what you want. The main deterrant is survival. I believe we become so concerned with what we have to do to survive that we lose focus and become willing to talk to anyone. We lose sight of our business objectives and accept the any potential prospect who comes through the door.

I can tell you first hand that I did this for years. In fact, 30 years later, I still find it hard to say "no" to a potential prospect. I have had to discipline myself to only focus on the "profile" prospects. I want to talk to people who are going to enhance my long term business objectives. If there is no rational reason to accept a case that is outside my business plan, then I need to walk away.

I have discovered this same principle applies to products I choose to represent. There has to be a rational business reason to spend time evaluating, understanding and eventually representing a specific product. I remember a way to state this problem—"If it walks like a duck, sounds like a duck—then it must be a duck." Not that there is anything wrong with ducks, mind you, but we need to be discerning and make good judgments.

Here's an example of where I blew it, big time. There was once an insurance carrier that sounded like this duck. I had seen proposals from this carrier several times in competition and had successfully defeated the product because I could show the illustration assumptions were unrealistic.

One day, I was approached to represent the carrier and I told them no. Unfortunately, my business associate really believed in the stories. He thought their assumptions were valid and tried to convince me. He could not do it. But, he continued and eventually, he wore me down and I agreed to show it to prospective buyers. The illustrations were so good that the buyers liked them and bought them.

I went to meetings and heard the insurance company tell wonderful stories about how they were doing all of their economic magic. I was skeptical, but they told the story with such enthusiasm and sincerity I began to doubt my own business principles. After several years of hearing the story and seeing the results, I eventually was able to articulate the story to others with some enthusiasm and sincerity. I overcame my skepticism and began to believe in the tooth fairy, too!

Unfortunately, when the balloon burst, my original skepticism and arguments turned out to be reality. There was no magic and the illustrations were nothing but misrepresentations based on wishful thinking. The lesson in this for me was to listen to my instincts.

DEVELOPING A FILTER

Anybody who is experienced and has seen the various scams and shams knows when something cannot work. As fiduciaries for our clients, regardless of the products we sell, we have to take responsibility for the quality of our work.

The only thing we have to sell is our reputation and integrity. People count on us to do our homework and represent products that will deliver what we say they will deliver. We have to use our instincts, contacts and best judgment to protect our reputation. As long as we keep the golden rule uppermost in our minds, we can never fall from grace with our clients.

The golden rule is not "them that has the gold makes the rules." The golden rule is that we always treat people in the same manner we want others to treat us. In other words, if you were in the client's place and had to make a decision, what would you do for yourself?

Your filter should help you build the courage and faith needed to always make the right decision. Once I learned to effectively choose between the people I want to do business with and those who are just busy work. Those skills have helped me in other areas of my personal and business life.

Now that we have looked at this filter, let's move on to the first phase of the sales process—the opening interview.

CHAPTER SEVEN

Opening The Case

O kay! Earlier, I said to practice. But what is there to practice? Let's look at the opening interview and see if there aren't some things that we can make repetitive.

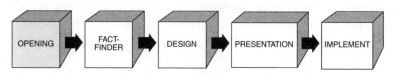

Think again about the professional athletes—the tennis pros, golfers, baseball players, skilled and gifted athletes who are unconscious competents. Do they practice? You bet they do. Why? Because they want to keep their skills sharp. They know they must maintain an edge or they will go flat and run the risk of losing their top standing. Professional salespeople must practice too.

Let's quickly review what we have learned. First, your filter must be in place. You know that you need to be efficient and effective, and have a backup filter for your main filter. You have learned that people do what they want to do when they want to do it. I mentioned also that the sale is always made in the factfinder and that each step of the process must be "on purpose." It must lead to the next phase of the selling system. So now, let's look at the opening interview—the second step in your sales system.

Opening the Case

Think about this! You have worked diligently for months to be positioned in front of this ideal prospect. But now the time has come and you have just gotten the go-ahead to conduct an opening interview. You remember that every sales/consumer psychologist in the world has told you that you have exactly 30 seconds to make a favorable impression. What are you going to say? What are you going to do?

I have found that most salespeople live with what I shall call the "Magic Words" syndrome. I believe it has plagued the sales profession forever. What do I say? What will work? When I first started selling, most of the sales books I read taught the magic words. I had to learn what to say, not why I had to say it or how to say it, but what to say. Memorize these words and you will successfully sell.

Now, I'd agree that knowing what to say is very important. After all, words are the only way we have of conveying our ideas and concepts. Imparting our knowledge is only 10% of the equation. "Knowing" people accounts for 90% of our sales skills. Are "magic words" important? I don't think so. The meaning and the compassion behind the words are more important than the words themselves.

Remember my sales axiom. If people only do what they want to do, what makes any of us think there is *anything* that we can say or do that will change or manipulate them into taking action? The key to communication is being able to convey ideas and concepts that open up the prospect's mind and then provide him with an opportunity to evaluate information at his own pace. Sales is a thought process, not an event.

When I first started selling insurance, I was faced with this "opening interview" complex. I constantly experimented with using the right phrases, the right ideas, the right concepts. I believed that I had to be quick enough, smart enough, shrewd enough to out talk the prospect. But I discovered something else. As I gained experience and also listened to the top sales people share their experiences, I realized that selling is relational. People respond to caring skills and caring words. I knew this instinctively. There is no one method which will work every time. Just as we differ in our tastes, ideas and ways of expressing ourselves, prospects are different, too. Therefore, sales-people need to be flexible in the way they deal with people. But does this mean the words need to be different?

I began to understand there are some commonalities which exist in every interview. As I studied them, I found what I really needed to do was to learn to confront the pertinent issues head on. I needed to be direct and speak to the prospect's specific fears. My tendency was to sidestep and avoid the tough issues and hope they would go away. After all avoidance is much easier than being direct—but only at first. Eventually, if the issues are real, you cannot avoid them.

Riskless Selling

If we dig deep enough, every prospect has real issues and real concerns. So, I realized I had a choice. I could use manipulation techniques and try to coerce prospects into doing what I wanted or I could deal directly with care and compassion. If I tried to manipulate, I risked my creditability. On the other hand, if I was too direct and confrontational, I risked offending them. Not everybody is ready for direct confrontation. They may not want avoidance, but they may not be ready for confrontation, either. So I decided I needed a direct approach that was not manipulative or confrontational. I call it *riskless selling*.

Riskless selling allows me to be as direct as the prospect will allow, yet still give him enough space to evaluate and think about his issues. Most importantly, it gives him an opportunity to go at his own pace. If people truly do what they want to do, then this method will meet their needs. No matter what type of person you are dealing with (direct or passive, outgoing or reserved) they all want enough space to feel like they are in control of their destiny. Nobody likes to feel as though they are being manipulated or controlled.

When I evaluated the profile of my best prospects, it was apparent that there was a specific list of issues and feelings most wealthy prospects had in common:

1. They virtually all had attempted to do some planning at one time or another.

2. They were concerned about the well-being of their family and wanted to make certain their economic condition was assured.

3. They wanted their businesses to continue which often meant paying off lines of credit or retiring long term debt.

4. They usually had a trusted advisor, someone outside their business to help them evaluate all of their options.

5. They wanted options, not ultimatums.

6. They were frustrated by the fast pace of change.

7. The complexity of the options made them feel helpless.

Getting the Factfinding Interview

When I first meet somebody, it is important for me to express my understanding of these issues but without necessarily making a major point of them. As I was learning to handle an opening interview, I experimented with various techniques and ways to get to the factfinding interview. Eventually, I discovered I had left the most obvious common characteristic off the list.

Every person, regardless of status and wealth, feels they are busy; too busy doing whatever it is that they do to spend much time planning. In fact, they are so busy being successful that they usually are reluctant to allocate any time to discuss these subjects with me. But any good salesperson knows we have to make lemonade out of lemons. I had to learn how to take this list of negatives and turn them into positives.

The basic rule of objections is that whoever controls the objection, owns the objection. I'll develop this more in the chapter on objections, but trust me, it's true! If you say the objection first, then the prospect is not likely to use it against you. However, once the client/prospect gains control of an objection, you play holy havoc getting around it. Think about the objections you have heard through the years. When the prospect owns the objection, he will use it until it doesn't work anymore. My objective is to always anticipate the objection and then use it in a positive way. Make the objection the very reason for him to do business with you.

After working with this list, it became apparent that being "too busy" was the very *key* I had been looking for. It became the central point in my opening interview. Of all the objections I ever got when I called up people for an appointment, "too busy" was the only one I had trouble handling. It always led to another call and perhaps still another, if I could get through. After all, people do what they want to do—right?

So I began to play around with being "too busy." But there is more. Take a look at the list of shared concerns again. What else is obvious from this list?

I think it is the desire to plan. Virtually every successful person has done some planning. I usually find their planning falls into one of three categories:

1. In some cases, they think their planning is entirely adequate and they have a false sense of security.

2. In other cases, they know they have not taken care of their tax obligations and succession/transition issues. They have grave concerns about this shortfall. As a result, they will sometimes go to their favorite attorney or accountant and proactively attempt to resolve their biggest issues.

3. Once in awhile, I will find someone who has done a significant job of planning. But often their planning was done several years ago and when they find out what is possible, they become angry that the planning they have done has become obsolete and they resent having to do it again.

In virtually all cases, there is *never* a coordinated plan which takes into consideration all of the planning issues. There are usually some big holes in the plan. Some of the most overlooked items are a business succession plan that will work, an incomplete tax financing plan, and inadequate preparation for retirement. There is very little thought given to the fairness and equity issues between family members except on a macro scale.

Denial is rampant. (By the way denial is *not* a river in Egypt.) There is a high probability that they have decided they cannot possibly keep up with the changes and have given up. Some have delegated the blame to their attorney or accountant. Others are confident their family will figure out how to handle the problems after they die. As a result, they don't want to do anything. The list is inexhaustible.

Here's the point. Many are convinced that they are helpless and unable to deal effectively with the complexity and magnitude of the planning problem. More importantly, remember, they are too busy anyway. So, it is easier to just ignore the problem and hope it goes away.

Having said all that, we are now face to face with Mr. (or Mrs.) Big. They have granted me an appointment and I have been given the ultimate challenge. I have to open their mind to what is possible in "30 seconds." But who's counting.

Let's review what we know about Mr. Big. We know he is often a success-driven person. He is energetic and competitive, and will delegate responsibility (but rarely authority). He is usually self-made, very intelligent and usually decisive. Under this thick veneer of projected competence, however is often fear and insecurity. He fears losing his business, his family, his self-esteem. He is often driven by hidden motives which aren't always readily apparent to those who know him best. There may be family problems, alcohol, drugs or workaholism. Quite often he has children who have problems stemming from neglect and psycological abuse.

There is a wall of pride, as big as the Great Wall of China and his mega accomplishments are often flawed by the family issues. There may be the proverbial dike with a hole in it. The plug is weak and ready to blow. He may be waiting for the right person to come into his life and help him resolve these major issues. But he may fear opening Pandora's box. Our job is to just listen and learn.

What we have to remember here is that most business owners are independent thinkers. They have often taken extreme risks to achieve all that they have. They are egotistical. Their belief in their own self-sufficiency is paramount. But they live in a paradox.

On the one hand, they want to be independent and ignore the heavy hand of the government. On the other hand, they know they need to solve these problems and they weigh heavily. They know it would be foolish to let a lifetime of success be destroyed because they were too stubborn to take the necessary steps. These people are planners and really hate the thought of losing what they have built, even if they are dead. The other side is their intense need to remain independent and not give into the system.

This very paradox is your opportunity. The fact that they are "too busy" is to your advantage. The fact that many of them have done some planning and realize it is probably inadequate works to your advantage. The fact they want a logical method to help them make a decision is also to your advantage. So how do you tap into this opportunity?

Here you are. You're in your meeting with your really great prospect and you are ready to start the process. But you've been there before and when you left the last few times, you intuitively knew you wouldn't be doing business together anytime soon. What did he say to you? Did he tell you he already has an agent? Or did he say he doesn't believe in insurance? Was he not ready to do anything just yet or does he have great advisors that handle everything?

You have heard it all before, haven't you? When this has happened to me, I leave frustrated and a little angry at myself. I know I should be able to do something or say something to let the prospect know what I can do for him.

Oh, what could I have said that would have worked, that would have gotten his attention? Where did I go wrong? How can I disturb this complacency and self-satisfaction? If left undisturbed, these prospects are open to undisclosed liabilities and potential family discord. As financial counselors, we possess many of the answers to their financial security, but they have the key to unlocking the door to their imagination. We have to find the right keyhole.

Earlier I mentioned that most wealthy prospects have done some planning and this can be intimidating for us. It's even more disheartening to find out they own substantial amounts of insurance already. We must remember that these "super" prospects feel they have already invested substantial time and energy to solve their problems and are skeptical that we can bring anything meaningful to the table. If they see us, it is usually out of courtesy. They generally dispatch us with the skill of a surgeon, a skill that has been developed through years of practice. "Talk to my controller," they say. Or, "Gee, I'll need to discuss this with my trusted attorney."

The net result is often the same—another 'good prospect' deleted from our inventory or put into the 'china egg' file.

But riskless selling can solve these problems. It doesn't have to be that way! You can disturb the most confident prospect to take action. But it requires patience and takes time to understand the dynamics of their thinking.

Truthfully, I think most salespeople are too hyperactive. They lack patience and don't allow the prospect time to decide what they want to do. The very personality characteristics of the salesperson that appeals to the type A/driven prospect are the very characteristics that cause the salesperson to give up in frustration when he can't get an immediate decision from the prospect.

Make no mistake about it, patience is KING! It takes a long time to grow an oak tree. It takes real skill and endurance to land a sport fish. Most big game fisherman tell me it can take up to 6 hours to land the big one on the deck. What makes us think it won't take a commensurate amount of time to bring these "super" prospects to a decision?

Now you might be thinking that you don't have "super prospects." But to an agent at any level of development, the "big case" is relative. If you have a really good case, the way to deal with the prospect is the same. In fact, sometimes a smaller case is harder to sell simply because the cost represents a larger percentage of their income. However, don't focus on the size of the case, focus on the sales dynamics.

The "Too Busy" Obstacle

For each prospect, the puzzle of caring and love is going to be different. But as I mentioned earlier, we do know they all share one basic trait—they are too busy! They have placed an inordinate demand on their time. Between their business and social obligations, their home life and personal time, their charitable desires, they are often overwhelmed by their life-style decisions. As a result, we represent yet another intrusion on their time. But here is our chance to turn those lemons into lemonade.

If they are too busy, and we know this is the case, then this is also their Achilles heel—their one weakness we can use to our advantage. On some level, they know they are vulnerable to the multiplicity of changes that the government has imposed on all of us. Sure, they have relied on their advisors to help them keep up with the changes. But every time they get together with their attorney, it costs $1,000 or more and then they have to do it again and again. If they need a quick answer ... over the phone ... it costs $75, and so on. Their penchant for avoiding these nit-picking bills opens a door of opportunity for us.

Our 'super' prospect might cynically ask us why we think we have all the answers. My response is very candid. We are idea merchants and facilitators, not technicians. My job is to stay on top of the new planning ideas and find competent advisors who can convert these ideas into workable solutions that will actually solve the problem. It is important to stress the teamwork nature of our business. Today, no one person or organization can be all things to all people.

The "Advisors are Too Busy, Too" Obstacle

Most 'super' prospects really don't understand the professional's dilemma. This is just another component to this "too busy" equation. The client may subconsciously realize, but not want to accept, the fallibility of their legal and accounting advisors. Good advisors are swamped with too much work! They have, in many instances, ceased being a planner and become just a scribe. The complexity of execution has converted most professionals into a transactional mode. Write a document, do a tax return, research a problem. Rarely, do they have time to call up and just brainstorm a problem. These advisors are *too busy* to really meet the unspoken expectations of their clients.

The closest some advisors get to being pro-active is holding client seminars to update their following on recent tax changes. Others might do a mass mailing which announces the tax changes that will apply across the board. These mailings are not specifically tailored to their clients. I have had many advisors tell me they have been trying to get Mr. Big in to do their wills/buy-sell/estate plan/etc., for months/years. They are so glad I could convince Mr. Big to do this. I believe they are being genuine when they say this.

It is important that we thoroughly understand the plight of the advisor. MDRT statistics show that less than 3% of member business leads are generated from referrals by attorneys or accountants. Yet, these advisors control some aspect of virtually every significant selling opportunity you will ever have. I find most agents view these advisors as the enemy. Frankly, I find that every major sale I have ever completed was with the advisor being actively involved. Why? Because I included them on every phase of the process. They were able to give input into the plan. They became the guy nodding their approval, instead of trying to shoot holes in my sale.

Face it! They are just like any of us. These advisors need to look good to the client to maintain their credibility. They must play a role of "importance" and be viewed as valuable. So what—why not let them look good to their client. It's a "win-win" situation for everyone. Do we care who is the hero? In some cases, I think we really do! The insurance companies have convinced us we need a standing ovation every time we do something good. Bring on the plaques! Let the advisor take credit for your ideas and initiative. If all you get is the commission, isn't that enough?

Rules of the Game

If you follow the rules of riskless selling, the only problem you have to resolve is how to deal with the prospect if the rules to the game change mid-game. Tell me the rules of the game and I'll tell you if I even want to play. As long as the game is fair and the rules are clearly defined, you can usually find a way to win. But, what often happens is that agents are so afraid of their own shadow that they avoid establishing the rules of the game, up front. When it gets down to the end, the close of the sale, the client often takes control. Remember, you cannot lose something you never had. Yet, I've seen agents hang on for dear life for fear they will lose the sale. Why do they hang on if they never had the sale in the first place? But just the thought of having the sale is enough to encourage most agents to keep trying. Unfortunately, having "nothing" doesn't pay the bills.

So, what does this have to do with opening the case, anyway? EVERYTHING! For you see, it is during this opening gambit and the subsequent factfinder that you make the sale. Think of it as a peg in a peg board. You are placing pegs in the board each time you get a commitment. These pegs are to hold each hat of commitment. These commitments are the most important part of the sale. They are the rules by which you play—managing client expectations, handling the specter of competition, converting the advisor to an ally. All of these rules become the way you *complete* the sales process. They make it possible to hold the prospect accountable. But, be very careful to not overcommit in the beginning to what you are going to do for them. It is better to promise a little less and deliver a little more than to fail to meet their expectations.

Okay! I promised I would share the Riskless Selling approach. So let's go.

The "Too Busy" Sales Track

We know that every meeting starts out with the rapport building. You know this part of the interview well! It's like I might visualize a mating dance. You walk in, saunter around the office, maybe sit down. You smile, they smile. You comment on the weather, your prospect agrees. You mention the friend in common, he says nice things about him. He tells you about his recent trip. You notice his trophies on the wall and compliment him on the nice fish, nice telephone, nice telephone pole, and finally, after what seems like hours, he starts to look bored and begins to wonder when you are going to say why are you here.

It is at this point you had better be ready with your 500mm salvo. Because the clock has started ticking and you have exactly 30 seconds to make a lasting impression. I figure this is the make it or break it time. So I lead with my best thought. I introduce the concept of being "too busy". I'll say,

"Mr. Smith, as you may know we work with a lot of successful business people like you and I have found they all share one major thing in common. May I share what I've learned from other successful business people like you?" (I always ask permission because it implies consent and gets them into the process.)

"I've found that they are so busy being successful—doing the things you have to do to keep their businesses going—that they have no time to pay attention to all of the changes going on in Washington. Do you ever feel overwhelmed by all of this constant change?"

Wait for his response. (This is one of those poignant pauses we hear so much about.) The response is never exactly the same, but it is always the *same*. Remember, selling is adversarial. He expects you to ask him to buy and is prepared to say no. But the paradox is he knows he should be doing something and really wants you to help them.

With "too busy," I see the tension of our meeting—of the moment—begin to recede as he relaxes. Sometimes the prospect will smile that knowing smile of agreement. The stress is reduced and a bond of friendship begins to form. Someone understands, he thinks. On some level, he knows I'm right and he knows he is vulnerable. As the meeting progresses, I will continue and share other common denominators.

"Mr. Smith, everyone we work with has a plan by design or default."

Design or Default

Remember, these type of prospects have all done some planning. But they are angry that the changes keep coming and nothing stays stable. If you don't have a will, then you die intestate. This is a plan and it is by default. If there is no buy/sell agreement, something is going to happen when one of the owners dies. So there is a buy/sell agreement but it just may not be in writing. Likewise, when someone retires, if there is no plan, they will still become old and need to cut back on working. So there is a plan. It just may not be the one they want.

Most often their plan has become one by default. What was a plan by design two years ago has become one by default because of this constancy of change.

This plays right into what the prospect has always known. But it is important for him to not feel any blame. You have given him a logical reason and he feels like he is not alone.

"Every plan has a price tag. In other words, there is a measurable economic impact of every plan. Our firm measures this economic pricetag of your plan by creating an economic model of how much your plan would cost if it were operational. We then create models of alternative plans, which may be better suited both financially as well as emotionally, based on your goals and objectives. These alternatives have a pricetag as well, and we can help you measure the differences. Have you ever determined the pricetag of your plan?"

Pricetags and Alternatives

What is the psychology of these points? First, being too busy gives the prospect a way out. It releases him from any guilt and responsibility he may feel. Being "too busy" is a good excuse for not having been able to keep up with the constancy of change. More importantly, it is something everyone experiences. By releasing the blame and guilt, people are more willing to accept the inevitable. It is easier to then find a reasonable way to deal with it. "Maybe," they think, "this person can help me!"

The second thing the prospect understands is default. He knows that he gets new business because of default. He takes advantage of others because of default. It is not hard for him to understand that his plan is being outdated. Again, default releases blame. It's no wonder he feels vulnerable. More importantly, he doesn't want to be a victim of default himself. Again, he can identify with these common denominators. But because it does not reflect on him personally, he can agree and accept what you are saying. You are giving them an "out." You are not threatening their self-esteem by telling them they are dumb or have made a terrible mistake.

The final point, I believe, clinches the deal. Every plan has an alternative. Alternatives are a great way for the prospect to not feel pressured. In the back of his mind he knows this is true. Consumer studies show that most consumers want to know what else is available. If you don't give it to him, then he will go to someone else.

We need to give the whole picture, not just a portion. If the prospect is going to trust you, then he has to feel you are going to tell him the whole story. The pricetag aspect puts it on a business basis. He can see a logical business approach to the problem. Identifying the pricetag makes sense to him and you are right! He doesn't know the pricetag of his plan. So the offer to determine the pricetag is appealing. But in the back of his mind he wants to know what it will cost.

If the client is unsophisticated or has a small business or small net worth, I leave the opening interview at this level. They always want to know what it will cost for us to prepare these economic models. So I use the three ways we get paid—referrals, commissions or fees. I tell the client most people don't like fees but if he would feel more comfortable paying fees, then we are happy to work that way and he can buy his products from someone else.

Three Circles of Wealth

In the more sophisticated situations, I shift to the Three Circles story. But there is a specific strategy for using this. Think for a minute about what we know regarding our prospect. Among all the things we know, we know he has advisors. He didn't build this successful business without an attorney or a CPA. So to think we can just come in and start working with him, without dealing with the two-headed dragon, is unrealistic.

The Three Circles story was designed to head off that objection. Remember, whoever controls the objection owns it. I want to own this objection. But notice too, that it takes a little time to set up the objection. We saw in the "too busy" story how to setup the "plan either by design or default." They are *too busy* being successful to look at alternatives.

Top sales professionals all create word pictures or tell a story. It is a powerful way to give a prospective buyer information. A word picture takes the abstract and makes it concrete, visual. We can just say what we mean, but it is often difficult for the listener to truly understand the full ramifications of what you have said. By creating a story, the listener can ascribe his own feelings and experiences to the story and identify with emotion and concepts. It brings meaning to what you are trying to say.

If the prospect has significant wealth, then I need to expand my story. I have already implanted the idea of being "Too Busy," "Design or Default," "Pricetags and Alternatives." Now I must tell them about the "Three Circles of Wealth." This story was designed for another reason besides heading off the advisor objection. It was designed to demonstrate the complexity of the financial tools the prospect has to choose from. By using the Three Circles, you can do a mini factfinder as part of your filtering system.

After the design and default and the pricetags comments, I say,

"Mr. Smith, when we have worked with business owners like you, I have found they have three primary areas where they invest considerable money. I call these the Three Circles of Wealth: *"Wealth Accumulation, Wealth Succession and Wealth Preservation."*

Each of these circles has unique investment and legal tools that are used by people like you to achieve their goals and objectives. In addition, we find that the people we work with are often spending thousands of dollars in each of the circles as they try to achieve their objectives." (I then draw three circles side by side É but not touching.)

"The Wealth Accumulation Circle represents all of the tools used to build wealth using the company dollars and your personal dollars. Pension plans, profit sharing, 401K, thrift plans, and nonqualified plans are all common tools we use to convert taxable income into capital. The strategies of the '80's are no longer the

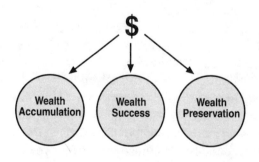

strategies of the '90's. Did you know 75% of all pension plans have been terminated because of the new laws? Most companies are switching to 401K plans because they are less expensive and allow the employee to participate. But the 415 limits have left the highly compensated employees with reduced benefits. We have developed ways to fill this deficiency."

"The Wealth Succession Circle represents all of the common tools used to pass ownership from one generation to another or from family management to professional management. These tools are buy/sell agreements, stock options, 303 stock redemptions and cross purchase agreements. But these tools can also include compensation planning, bonus structures, sales compensation and fringe benefits. You can diversify your holdings in your company today TAX-FREE. Would you like to pull out 30-50% of your company's value ... in cash?

"The Wealth Preservation Circle refers to all of the tools used to pass assets from one generation to another at the lowest cost. They include charitable trusts, QTIPs, marital deduction planning and liquidity concerns. We can help you discount your taxes 80-90% using your corporation's cash flow. We can create tax-free capital with tax-free income. This wealth preservation is done estate tax and income tax-free.

Now comes the fun! The prospect is probably thinking that he is paying several advisors to help them do all of this. But before he can express this objection, let's turn it into a positive. Whoever controls the objection, owns it.

"Mr. Prospect, we commonly find that the business owner has several advisors they rely on to help them manage their three circles of wealth. You have an attorney and an accountant, don't you? What about a financial planner? An insurance agent?"

By asking these questions, it keeps you in a factfinding mode and prevents the prospect from turning your question into an objection. As long as you are not threatening him with your questions, you can get a lot of information. As soon as you turn your questions from advisor to salesman, you have lost the ability to factfind. It is important you continue to seek information. Remember, this is riskless selling.

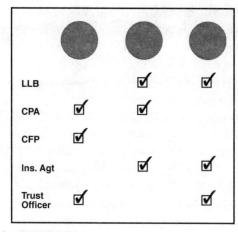

Once I get the answers I am looking for, I say,

"Mr. Prospect, what happens is that these advisors are so busy being successful that barriers are erected between the circles which prevent effective communication. The resulting inefficiencies are created because the left hand doesn't always know what the right hand is doing."

Depending upon the response you get, this line of thinking can achieve different objectives. In some cases, the advisors are talented and competent. You will want to meet them and start developing a relationship with them. The Three Circles presentation gives you an opportunity to work as a facilitator to bring all the parties together to create the efficiencies you spoke of.

In other situations, you learn that the prospect doesn't really like their attorney/CPA, etc. This creates a referral opportunity for your team of advisors. You win either way. I have found that the prospect rarely will say no to this line of reasoning. He instinctively knows that there are areas where he

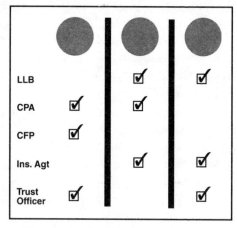

could be more efficient and effective. You have given him a logical reason to let you work with their team to pull things together.

"This lack of coordination between these advisors has created an opportunity for us to work with people like you. Because the advisors are so busy and often are unable to keep up with the changes, our firm teams up with them. Often we find that we look at things a little differently. We attempt to combine these circles like this ... (Now I draw them like Olympic rings.)

"Notice how each circle overlaps the other ones. This rep-

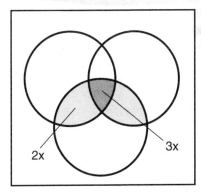

resents the many opportunities to combine tools and solve common problems with the same dollars. We can achieve double and triple duty dollars in some instances. There are ways to combine tools and use them in more than one circle. You have already made the decision to invest substantial dollars in the solutions to these problems. If I can show you an acceptable way to get double or triple duty from your existing dollars, would you be interested?"

The whole point of this explanation is to demonstrate that creative planning can convert the dollars that the prospect is already allocating to the various solutions, to get more "bang for his buck." I call the place where the circles overlap three times— triple duty dollars. The place where the circles overlap twice is double duty dollars. It would be a rare prospect who can resist seeing if he can get more for his money. All you can really do is make your offer enticing. But it has to make sense—it has to be real. In other words, you must learn the tricks of the trade and be able to apply them.

At this point, either the prospect is going to agree to let you see his planning ... OR ... you will get some objections. Most often, he will ask you how you get paid.

How We Get Paid—The Second Filter

This is an important part of the first interview and often overlooked. "If you don't work for free, how do you get paid?" The prospect knows you don't work for nothing. You know he is fee sensitive with his attorney and CPA. He also doesn't want to buy anything new so you can get a commission. By offering to do this analysis and provide an overview of his existing plan, you need to set his expectations properly. I tell them that I am willing to do the analysis as a way to build the relationship.

"Mr. Prospect, we will look at your current plan and come back to you with a report that will show you how you might combine tools to achieve better efficiencies. We want an opportunity to earn the right to do business with you. We are willing to invest in the relationship to see if there are ways we can help.

"If we discover ways to improve your position and can demonstrate one or more meaningful ways to save you money or achieve better efficiencies, is there any reason you wouldn't do business with us?"

This approach allows us to turn the proverbial lemons into lemonade! We have overcome the advisor objection and offered to review his planning for the right to build the relationship. Most good business people want ideas. They don't want to pay for them.

Bruce Etherington, from Toronto, Canada, calls this "the deal before the deal." This is the second filter. It comes after you have done the mini-factfinder to determine if you want to do business with this person. Remember, your first filter protected your magic box. It brought you to this place. But that filter is not enough. If you want to increase your productivity, you need to be more discreet. You need to find out exactly what opportunity exists and whether you want to pursue it.

The second filter will save you a lot of time and heartache. If the prospect is not willing to agree to the deal now, then he certainly won't agree to it later. We can waste a lot of time, energy and effort helping people, only to find out the deal has changed. We need to get a commitment up front. We need to set the expectations properly. You can't lose something you never had. It is wishful thinking to be-

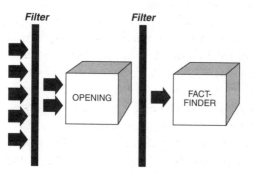

lieve that this prospect will feel obligated after you have done some work. Find out now who he does business with and whether you have a chance.

It is important to establish up front how you are going to work together. This is the foundation for your long term business relationship. If you set the deal properly, you will have a beneficial relationship. But if you fail to do it properly, then you may be disappointed.

Assume the prospect doesn't ask how you get paid ... then bring it up! Remember, this is your second filter. This is how you make certain your first filter was accurate. You need several commitments to place this prospect into your magic box. First, you need to know he has a need. Second, you need to know if he can afford to do what you recommend. Third, you need to find out if he will do business with you. Finally, you need to determine if he can make a decision.

Two Profits

I call this the "Two Profits." I don't mean Elijah and Elisha either. I say, "Mr. Prospect, I think it is important for you to know how we get compensated. Our firm works on both fees and commissions. We have found that there are two ways we can charge fees—retail and wholesale. Our retail fee is based on billing you our standard hourly rate. It covers our overhead and profit—much like your CPA firm or lawyer. That way, if you decide you want to purchase a product, you can use anybody you want. You pay us our profit for doing the analysis and then you pay another profit to whoever you buy your products from.

"If you elect to use us on a wholesale basis, we will only charge the actual "hard costs" we invest in your study. We simply eliminate the profit portion of the fee. We know a firm like yours purchases a lot of commissionable products during the course of the year? For instance, you purchase group benefits from a broker, your 401k plan probably pays a commission, and you have other benefits as well. Your representative gets a fee for servicing the account. But, what other services do they provide? We can use these commissions to offset the costs of doing this study. In addition, we find that sometimes additional products are required to complete the job you have started. By doing business with our firm, it offsets our overhead for doing the analysis. Our profit can come from any commissions you would pay ordinarily to another broker. So you basically have a choice, Mr. Prospect, you can either pay the profit once or twice."

The "I have an Agent" Obstacle

What if the prospect has an existing agent? Most successful business owners, especially if the company is substantial, will have somebody they have bought insurance from in the past The question is, who is the agent? In some cases the agent will be a very professional and talented advisor. Why waste valuable time competing against a good agent? There is a lot of business out there.

On the other hand, it may make sense to go head to head because the client represents a prestigious case and there will be outstanding contacts generated from the case. However, "the deal before the deal" needs to address exactly how the prospect is going to make this decision. If you are not comfortable you will be fairly treated, then exit stage right.

The final alternative is to do joint work on the case. There may be reasons why neither of you wants to compete with each other. But joint work is difficult and requires a firm agreement up front.

I have found most people are loyal to their current advisors—especially their life insurance agents. More importantly, you want this same loyalty shown to you. So it is important to handle this problem carefully. If you attack the other agent, it could backfire. You might blow your creditability. Many people are turned off by any signs of greed. Ruthless criticism will never win many friends.

Silence is often a more potent killer. My mother told me, "If you can't say something nice about someone, don't say anything at all." When someone intentionally attacks another, I find myself questioning their motives. In a sales interview, it is important to put your best foot forward. If criticism is warranted, there will be time for it at another date.

But by the same token, it is important to differentiate between your services and those of the other agent. This is why you need to have a clear understanding of your image. What is your business philosophy? How do you convey this in your business and to your clients?

Three Terrific Truths

I have utilized three philosophies during the years. First, whether I made the mistake or the client made the mistake, I am responsible. Therefore, I feel I should make it right. Even if this costs me some profit on the case, or causes me to actually lose money, it is worth it to know I did the right thing.

The second "truth" is ... don't ever burn bridges. Life is too short to go out and stink up your marketplace with egotistical pride. I've seen agents respond with foolish pride and "win" the battle. But people never forget. You have the choice to make a big thing out of a small matter or accept the responsibility and let it go. Tom Peters has said repeatedly that one unhappy ex-client will tell everyone they can about you. You don't need that kind of help.

The third rule relates to problem solving and complaints. Get on it ... NOW! I think about how I feel when I want something done. I can't relax until I know the solution is in process. I think others feel the same way. Develop a sense of urgency to resolve problems quickly. I will confront anything which is detrimental to me, my business or the well being of my clients. This has always been a successful strategy.

Never, Never, Never Quit

I have found many of the prospects I approached and cases I lost five years ago are open to doing business today. The solution or agent they chose over me didn't work out. They liked my ideas but the timing wasn't right and timing is everything. Too often the case goes to the agent who was in the right place at the right time. Let's look at how this comes about.

Many of the best prospects started in their garage years ago. They became successful and have enjoyed dramatic growth during the last few years. They hired their neighborhood attorney, and local CPA to get them started. Somehow, their agent met Mr. Smith and sold some term insurance and group health. He's been there ever since.

It is not unusual for Mr. Smith to replace both his attorney and CPA during the years. As his business has grown, his needs have changed and he made the appropriate decision. The survivor is the life insurance agent. Why? Life insurance is perceived as a product, a commodity, not a service. Most buyers feel they need to get the best price and they deal on trust. If you can disturb the trust, then you have a chance to obtain the business.

If Mr. Smith is a loyal, honest person, he will admit to you in your opening interview that he has an agent. When this happens, I'll say, "I'm not surprised to hear you have an agent." Remember the 3 R's? This is the 'repeat.' "In fact, I would have been surprised if you didn't (reassure). But what I have discovered is most people outgrow their agents (resume).

"As the laws change and the specific applications are better understood, these old line agents are often passed by. They aren't able to keep on top of these changes. I spend four to six weeks each year in continuing education. I do this to keep from falling behind and having the same thing happen to me."

The best clients will almost always have an agent. If you don't learn to handle this objection, then you will be passing by a lot of business. Unfortunately for them and fortunately for us, even though they have an agent, the work has rarely been done. And even if it has been done, it is probably outdated or even sloppy. Why accept "I have an agent!" as the final word? Find out for certain they are doing the job.

We have all heard the "second opinion" response. If insurance companies make doctors do it, then shouldn't you do it as well? But if canned answers are insulting, if I come across too slick and polished, then the client may feel uncomfortable. The best answer is the honest answer.

"Mr. Smith, I mentioned early in our meeting that most people are too busy to pay attention to these changes. I can assure you, if you allow me to review your program—two things will happen. First, you will get a competent review and a list of areas for you to reconsider. And second, I promise I will not recommend changes unless I can prove to ALL of your advisors it makes sense. All I want is an opportunity to earn your confidence and loyalty. And just as with your current agent, I hope you will come to value us as one of your most trusted advisors."

Again, the theory is to get the chance. Once you have it, then you'd better do something professional with it.

CHAPTER EIGHT

Nothing But The Facts

Wouldn't you like to know why people buy? I would! It would make life as a salesperson so much easier. There is substantial research that proves you can read minds by watching which way the eyes move, or by mirroring behaviors. But that seems somewhat manipulative to me. Wouldn't you rather enjoy the discovery of the person within your prospect? Let the prospect go where he wants to go and do what he wants to do. After all the prospect is going to do that anyway. He will be happy and you will have a long relationship.

The opening interview is designed to develop an open ended discussion with your prospective client about his hopes, desires and goals. If he agrees to let you explore his alternatives, then you have taken the biggest step towards a sale. Once you get through the opening interview and he has given you permission to do the factfinder, you are virtually home free.

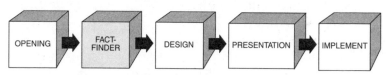

The factfinder is a wonderful time to learn what you can about how your new client thinks and acts. He has given you unlimited license to

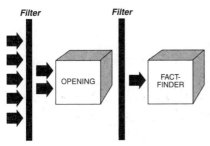

explore his past, present and future. You can ask questions about the decisions he has made and how he feels about those decisions. What would he do differently if he had a second chance? You can ask him how he feels about insurance, why he bought it and how he determined the amount he wanted to purchase.

The only thing you cannot do is sell. Stay away from any decision-making statements. Do not, under any circumstances, undermine the confidence you are building. Not too long ago, a business owner, Pete, came to my office. He wanted to start planning for retirement. I knew his attorney and in a discussion with the attorney, I found out that this business owner really needed a business succession plan. In fact, the entire subject was on the table.

When Pete and I got together, I immediately started talking about the business succession plan. I totally bypassed the reason Pete came to see me. To add insult to injury, he told me how much insurance he owned. I explained to him that this coverage wasn't nearly enough and convinced him to sign applications for $1,000,000 of coverage. We scheduled the exam while he was in the office. He left and I was pleased because I had averted a potential disaster for his family.

The next week he canceled the doctor's appointment and never took the physical. Fortunately, I was in a group where I saw him regularly. I took him aside and asked what happened. After a few moments of awkward silence, he told me that I had pushed him into something he was not prepared to do. In fact, he had come to me for an entirely different reason than what we had talked about. He then told me I was like every other agent he had ever dealt with and was disappointed in me.

Naturally, I quickly backpedaled and apologized for my error. I explained that I only took that course of action because his attorney had suggested I needed to take action. He understood and said we could try again. The next meetings were more successful. Ultimately, he bought the insurance he needed, but when he wanted to do it and only in the amount he wanted to buy.

I made the sale in the factfinder, but not because I pushed the solution. Rather, it was because I had all of the facts and could see the big picture. You need to have a strategy for the factfinder. You need to know how you are going to get from the beginning to the end. It is all part of the process.

There is a selling axiom for all of us to remember. Once you emerge from the opening interview, you have made the sale! All of the statistics from my research show that nearly 90% of all factfinders will result in a sale. You don't know what you have sold, but you have sold something. At this point, it is your case to close *IF* you do the right job.

Remember the importance of your filters. If you have prospected properly, if you have done the opening interview properly, if you have done the "deal before the deal," then you will make a sale. Your only risk now is that you may make a mistake that knocks you out of the case.

The basic principle of the factfinder is just what it says; you are gathering facts. The purpose of gathering facts is to restate them to your prospect in a clear and concise manner. The purpose is *NOT* to sell a product. Although a sale may very well be the outcome, it is important to have a consultant's mindset during the fact gathering period.

Your most important job is to be objective. You must listen with both ears to the information as you ask the question, "Why?" There are really two reasons. First, the answers are important to understanding the client's long term objectives. But equally important, are the answers that will lead you to the next questions. By hearing what the client says, you can find the thread to the central issues in his life. By listening, the client will tell you not only how to sell him, but what to sell him. You must believe that you would not be there unless the client wanted to do something. You must figure out what that something is.

It is important that you do not shame or blame your prospective client. Don't be judgmental when you hear the answers. There are obviously right and wrong ways to do things. But in the factfinder, you are just trying to find out what he has done and why. If you are critical or judgmental, you're likely to discourage your prospect and turn them off to the process. Be kind and understanding. He is just doing the best he can with what he knows. Our job is to enlighten him about what is possible so he can make a good decision.

Another important aspect of the factfinder is not to be helpful—yet. Answers to the prospect's questions should be postponed until later. If we come up with the answers too quickly, he won't trust us. If you have the urge to be too helpful, ask yourself why? Very often it is only to build yourself up in the prospect's eyes, often at his expense. So, postpone giving answers. It is hard to refrain from being helpful, especially if he is asking questions. But you can just say that *"we will get to those issues later."*

The key to the factfinder is to make the prospect "feel" the questions. Ask him hard questions that take thoughtful answers. By making him dwell on the answers for awhile, he will often come up with important insights.

Speaking of hard questions, we must remember to emphasize the soft facts. There are hard facts and soft facts. The hard facts are the numbers. But the hard facts are only a snapshot of a specific period in time. They give us the information we need for the economic models. But the soft facts give us the priorities and objectives. It is through the soft facts that we are able to determine the prospect's real needs and help him discover what he really wants to do.

Learn to ask soft fact questions. Your ability to be a good consultant is dependent upon this skill. Here are some basic rules of asking soft fact questions:

1. Make the prospect feel the problem
2. Let him gain a sense of the issues and the cost of not taking action
3. Don't fill the silence—let him answer the questions
4. Don't lead him in his answers

It is critical that the prospect has time to process his own answers. I think agents are so focused on making the sale that they often miss the real reason agents do what they do. Don't we sell to help people? If you blow through the process, all you've done is made a sale. In some cases that is enough, but there is usually so much more there. Why let the opportunity go by because you need to get on to the next prospect?

Here is an example of a series of questions you might ask about estate and business planning:

- How do you feel about paying estate taxes?

- How much tax would be acceptable?

- Which assets would you want your family to sell to finance the tax?

- What if you were unable to get a loan?

- What would happen if there was no market for your company at the time you had to sell it?

- Who is the logical president to take over your company?

- What training and experience has the replacement had?

- If something were to happen to you tonight, what are the threebiggest problems your family would face?

When you are asking 'soft facts' questions, it is almost as if you are building a doctor/patient relationship. You want to gain their respect and trust. You want them to count on you for the answers. You want them to confide in you and feel that you will treat their problems and issues with the highest level of respect and integrity.

Remember, you are trying to create an atmosphere of safety and security. They have never been here before and your job is to guide them through the treacherous waters to safety. Your factfinder is the beginning of a nine step process that will lead them to a decision. These are the steps you should follow:

1. Obtain permission to ask questions

2. Gather the facts

3. Demonstrate the scope of the problems

4. Measure the price tag of their current situation

5. Show them alternatives that they should consider

6. Allow them time to think about it

7. Show them a prospective implementation schedule

8. Ask them if they are ready to make a decision

9. Ask them when they would like to start implementation

If you follow this outline, your probability of making a sale increases substantially. Once you have used this process effectively and really adopt it as your own, you will never go back.

I think you need to share these steps with your client. He wants to know what is going to happen and what to expect. The chart below is one that we use to effectively convey the process.

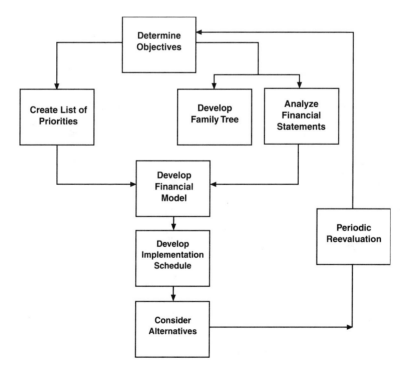

People like to know where they are going and how they are going to get there. Most people are controlling, and need to feel like they are in control of the process. If you keep it a mystery, they will tire of the process and quit. Tell them what you are going to do and how long it will take. Remember, they are still tentative about the outcome of this process. They need time to adjust to the steps. You need to let them become comfortable with what you are going to do. Show them you are working a system and have done this many times before. They will gain confidence from knowing you are skilled at what you do.

The entire purpose of the factfinder, besides learning about the prospect's needs and how you can help him, is to build an attitude of exploration and investigation. By getting him to explore and investigate his alternatives, you move him into the next phase of the sales process—negotiation.

If you are going to build economic models to show the prospect how his plan works, then you need to understand his plan. You have to be able to capture the details in such a way that you will be able to show exactly how much it is going to cost the prospect if his plan were to be implemented today. Once you can do this, then showing him the alternatives, and the potential savings, is easy.

If you blow this opportunity by making any of the major factfinding mistakes, you probably will have lost any opportunity to sell this prospect. This is where most joint cases fall apart. The *introducing* agent has taken the case too far and already exposed many of the strategies that should be considered. Instead of leading the prospect along the path, the *introducing* agent has forced the sale and alerted the wary prospect to the danger. When the *joint* agent arrives on the scene, the damage has been done and the sale has been blown. It would take a Herculean job to put Humpty Dumpty back together again.

Two Rules of Factfinding

Before we look at five common errors made in factfinding, we need to consider two fundemental rules that will make factfinding more effective.

First, never, never, never use the 'I' word in the factfinder. By

making insurance an issue in the factfinder, you blow all credibility as a consultant. You become the enemy because you are
trying to sell the prospect before he is ready to buy. The ideal
strategy is to make the prospect say the 'I' word first. In fact, that
is the rule. Whoever says the 'I' word first *loses*. By that I mean,
if the prospect says the I word first, then he has determined that
insurance is a viable product and makes sense for him to investigate. If, on the other hand, you use it first, then you have put your
cards on the table. If the prospect is ready, then he may buy. But
if he is not ready, then he is likely to run for the hills. He won't
return your calls and he is unlikely to give you another chance.

This is probably a controversial position. But I believe every
potential prospect has a bias about insurance. Unless you know for
sure what his feelings are about insurance, you run the risk of introducing insurance too early in the conversation.

Our fear, of course, is that the prospect might buy from someone else or that we will be perceived as being dishonest. But remember, in the opening interview you did the "deal before the deal."
If you did this properly, the prospect has already agreed to buy the
product from you if it is needed. All you have to do now is wait for
the right time to bring up the subject. Better yet, let him bring it up.
Prospects are smart, and they will understand their problems if you
show them economic models that demonstrate their costs. They
will eventually be open to alternatives that solve the problems.

Another problem that is created if you introduce insurance too
soon is it takes the focus off the alternatives approach. As a result,
the relationship becomes solution driven instead of problem driven.
You may want to review Chapter 4 and the problem/solution scale.
Insurance is such a wonderful solution that it really sells itself in
the right environment. Your strategy needs to be one of problem
identification. Load up the wagon and you only enhance the probability of making a significant sale. If you bring the solution into
focus too soon, you run the risk of losing the sale or reducing the
size of it. Let the client guide this part of the process.

You must remember that insurance is a financial commodity.
As a commodity, it is price driven and the prospect will want to
compare prices. This often means extra work and potential risk.

However, when insurance is presented to the client as a service and perceived as such, the client will buy from you with very few questions about price.

In the legal profession, the factfinding process is called discovery. Each side has to interview the various players and ask questions. They piece together the information and ultimately get the big picture. The power of self-discovery is awesome. It plants on the "shelf of the mind" the importance of the solution because they discovered it for themselves. We don't want to rob our prospects of this opportunity.

Rule Number Two of factfinding is "Don't Hurry the Sale." As long as you don't make a tactical mistake, you will always make a sale. Virtually the only thing you can do wrong is to hurry the process. It is important to have the confidence that underlies this truth. If you have confidence in your ability to help your client, then your confidence will be transferred to your client. This is the heart of riskless selling.

If you are having difficulty accepting rule number two, ask yourself this question, "Why would your prospect give you all of the information you requested, allow you to probe personal issues and participate in the negotiation process, only to say no?" It doesn't make sense. If you allow the prospect to understand his own problems, negotiate his own solutions and design his own implementation schedule, why wouldn't he buy?

You must trust this rule from the start. If you have confidence in *you*, then the prospect will have confidence in you. That is why having a sales process that you use over and over again is so important. Without the process, you will appear disorganized and incompetent. Your trustworthiness depends upon your process.

Let's look at common errors agents often make in the factfinder.

Overpromising, Underdelivering

When I look back through the years, I have been guilty of this. I get caught up in the circumstances and jump to a conclusion. Instead of being patient and looking thoroughly at all of the facts, I seize one or two "big" items and give a solution. I call this over-promising.

Then, I am put on the spot. I have to deliver. But what I never understood was that this is not a win/win situation. If I deliver, then I have given the client what he expected and I win. If I don't deliver, then I lose. So I have toned down my style and I don't set the expectations too high or too early. I let the process flow and wait until all of the facts are on the table.

I think I was trying to be a hero and show how valuable I could be to the client. Now, I wait for the facts and let others participate in the process. The results are the same but the perception is different. Instead of delivering what I said we could, we now deliver more than what was promised. The client is happier. On the downside, if the savings is less than anticipated it is not as painful. It is better to underpromise and overdeliver because then you are always the hero with little or no downside.

Making Statements that Cannot be Substantiated

This error is similar to overpromising. However, the root is different. Here, the agent is just plain wrong. Instead of doing the research and making sure of the facts, the agent jumps out with a stupid statement and blows his credibility. This usually happens because of impatience and inexperience. The only way to avoid this problem is to make certain you know all of the facts and the issues before you start to speak. Sometimes it is painful to wait. But in the end it is smart to wait until you are certain about your facts.

Pushing Too Fast

Here is the heart of riskless selling. If you start moving too fast the client will put on the brakes. I'm reminded of training a dog to walk on a leash. Remember how they dig in their heels and you have to pull them down the street? Dogs do this because they are afraid and the leash upsets them. Proper training techniques say that you should just let the dog wear the collar and leash for a few days to get used to it. Then start guiding them.

Clients have much the same temperament. If you let them walk around a while and get used to the leash, then they are happier when you start to guide them. Pushing too fast occurs when you start pressing for a decision, using the 'I' word too soon, or offering solutions when you should be dealing with problems. The sales process has its own timetable and requires strict sensitivity and adherence.

I have discovered through the years that top sales people instinctively recognize the nuances of this process and are able to gauge the proper speed. By guiding the client through the process at his speed, we retain his confidence and loyalty. But this guidance takes patience and perseverance.

Not Working With the Advisor.

This error can be fatal to your sale. It is easy to overlook the advisor and his importance to the client. But most successful business owners know the value of counsel. Would you be willing to make a big expenditure without getting some independent feedback? I don't think so! A good CPA or LL.B. is too critical to a client's long term success to just pass them by. But the interesting thing is that many of these advisors have not successfully addressed many of the problems we uncover. Another aspect is our perspective. As underwriters, we often view the issues from a different angle and bring a new viewpoint.

I have had many advisors through the years tell me that they were glad I got involved because they had been unable to get the client to take action. Sometimes the confidence we have is only the result of the confidence we have gained. These can be dangerous waters and may require the experience of another agent. I strongly urge you to consider joint work when you recognize you are in new waters. This is a great way to learn and earn. Think of it as tuition. It is only one case, not a marriage. You can take your experience and use it many times over in the years to come.

Not Being Responsive

Benign neglect is a sad commentary on the sales process, but it happens. I know from my own experience, you get busy, other issues arise, you aren't altogether certain what to do. There are many reasons, but the result is you fail to follow through and the client loses confidence.

A personal philosophy is the only way to solve this problem. You must do what you say you are going to do regardless of the cost. Your reputation is all you have to market. If you do not do your best 99% of the time, it will catch up with you. In those cases where you don't want to follow through, you need to be honest and just tell the prospect that you are not able to help him at this time.

Frankly, there is no excuse for not doing what you say you are going to do. Sometimes we just have to reach down and gut it out.

CHAPTER NINE

Why People Buy

The question salespeople probably ask the most is, "How did you meet this prospect?" The second most asked question is, "What did you say to get him to buy?" Magic words are a myth. Yet salespeople are always looking for the right words. This concept of "why people buy?" is at the *heart* of the sales process. But maybe, we are looking for the right answers in the wrong place. Instead of trying to find the magic words, maybe we should be seeking the right attitude.

I want to explore this subject with you and see if we can't build a mutual understanding about the natural process of converting ignorance to knowledge. It is my belief that the reason most people *do not buy* is because they do not understand—they are ignorant. However, I have to be open to the fact that I am equally ignorant—about their needs. Sales is really about communication, and that communication revolves around the buyer's needs and your understanding of his alternatives. Here is my definition of selling:

> **Selling is the process of developing a mutual understanding of the problems and the alternatives faced by the prospect. A *sale* occurs when I have a solution that the prospect will buy.**

WHY PEOPLE BUY

Most salespeople usually enter into a sales dialogue with a pre-set bias. Our knowledge is based on our experiences and we ascribe to the buyer our own estimate of his problems and his need for our solution. This bias can turn our dialogue into a monologue.

It is almost like the computer and a software program. The hardware, the computer itself, has no value unless it has a program that it can operate. But the program functions on input according to the bias of the programmer. If the programmer has the wrong formula, then the output will be wrong. These mistakes are often referred to as "bugs." If our *sales* software has been programmed by years of personal experiences, then our program may have "bugs" as well. Some of our experiences have been very healthy but some have been dysfunctional. Our output (communication) is the result of our software's ability to process the information (any input and stored experiences).

Does this sound familiar? You are there in the interview, listening to a client explain his situation. When he says the "magic words" (buy/sell, estate taxes, retirement), I often tune out and start thinking of my next response. I may miss the nuances of his concerns because I am processing where to go next because he triggered my thought process with key words.

I am reminded of a time early in my career when I approached a very successful senior level executive who indicated he was willing to help me. I tried to explain a very complicated financial transaction (minimum deposit life insurance) used to fund retirement benefits for large corporations. I felt awkward and ill-at-ease in the discussion. I was intimidated by his stature and I was not totally comfortable with my knowledge of the transaction.

During the discussion, he asked very pointed questions but I heard them as objections to the idea. When he offered these questions, I responded defensively, thinking he was trying to find fault with my idea. After a couple of attempts, he stopped and asked me why I was defensive. I tried to explain that I was attempting to clarify this concept and his objections were making me uncomfortable. He then explained that I wasn't listening to him. He wanted to understand this idea, so he was asking questions for information, not giving reasons against my idea.

He pulled me up short because I was being defensive when he asked me questions. My defensiveness was the result of my prior programming, wasn't it? This executive's willingness to confront me reprogrammed my software. If that experience was stored properly and reaccessed in similar situations in the future, I could say I learned from that interaction.

I believe we can be our own worst enemy in the sales process. If we have utilized our filter properly and eliminated potential prospects who are not compatible with our magic box, then we have gone a long way towards our eventual goal, achieving sales success. *We have a choice.* We can reprogram our "thinker" so it will gather input from the prospect and give output that will help the buyer to buy, or we can adhere to our predisposition and react based on our experiences.

Let's talk about our programming. From my own personal experience, I don't think there is just one single reason why people buy something. If people really do what they want to do, when they want to do it, then there are probably many reasons, as there are people, why they take action. But I have discovered that there are predictable patterns of behavior that people invariably follow. If we can understand those patterns, learn to recognize them, and learn to respond ethically and rationally, we can predict their likely behavior. This then allows us to move our prospect down the learning curve. By anticipating his reactions to the sales process, we are in a better position to help him do what he ultimately should do.

Is this manipulative selling? I don't believe so. When I hear sales psychologists talk about the buying behaviors, I am ultra sensitive to the manipulative elements that may be suggested. Manipulation occurs when the influencer (usually us) causes the prospective buyer to do something he does not want to do, using artificial gimmicks or tricks. The "fatal alternative" is a benign example of this. "Would you rather meet Friday at 7:00 PM or Thursday at 8:00 PM?" Assumed consent is an example of manipulative selling techniques. I always ask permission. When someone jumps the gun with me, I will stop him and ask him what he is doing. Do you like it when someone sells you using manipulative techniques?

Other techniques of manipulation are guilt, shame, fraud or

other equally offensive behaviors to cause the prospect to take action. It is no wonder the image of the insurance agent backing the hearse up to the door is a stereotypical description of our trade.

There is an important rule of selling that I follow. It allows me to guide the discussion. *I never ask a question I don't know the answer to.* By relying on what I know and adding to it what I don't know, the prospect and I move together towards the ultimate goal—understanding the problems and the alternatives. I call this achieving the predictable result.

What is the predictable result? If you had perfect knowledge, you knew all of the inputs and all of the reactions, you could predict the outcome. Because there is a predictable pattern of behavior for most problems, once you understand the problems and the objectives, you can predict the outcome. If a wealthy estate holder says he is not interested in giving much of an inheritance to the kids, the result is predictable. You will have to overcome his understanding of inflation and taxes before he will consider any planning solutions. If a prospect owns a business and plans to retire, it is predictable that you will have problems if he or she has not yet started any succession planning. If he says, "I think I will buy term and invest the difference," you know you have to demonstrate the economics of life insurance at the older ages. You know too, that he needs to understand his need for insurance after retirement.

The patterns are usually the same. We must learn to recognize the patterns and develop a catalog of responses that are appropriate. Unless we learn to recognize these patterns, we will always be on the defensive, trying to find effective arguments to overcome his objections. If, on the other hand, we are congruent, honest and ethical in our relationships, we can ultimately help him do what he wants to do.

To me, persuasion is the effective exchange of information between the knowledge worker and the receiver. This exchange is meant to cause the prospective buyer to re-evaluate his own issues and perhaps change his mind based on new input and understanding. However, it may result in the knowledge worker learning new information about his buyer and ultimately causing a better outcome for both the buyer and the seller.

WHY PEOPLE BUY

Every salesperson accepts the fact that knowledge is power. Imparting knowledge to someone in a way that allows him to process the information and perhaps change his mind is communication—not manipulation. I think you will see that as we develop these thoughts further, sales can be a constructive process of continual education. If we allow the prospect enough time to think through his concerns and fears, he will take the appropriate action. After all, he always does what he wants to do.

Trusting the Principle

We need to have freedom in our relationships to communicate honestly and openly with our prospects. If our communication is tainted with unethical or selfish motives, then selling ceases to be a noble profession and becomes fraudulent. Professional salespeople take great pride in knowing they have benefited their clients through ethical and honest selling methods. Is there any one of us who wants to have his reputation soiled by using improper tactics? I don't think so!

Having said all of this, let's look at an ethical approach to dealing with people who are tentative or slow to act—an ethical approach that allows you to improve your probability of success, yet still allows the prospect to retain his dignity and self-will. After all, if your job is to make something happen, then you need to develop skills that will increase your probability of success. If nothing happens, then you are out of business.

Think about a recent sales experience where your prospect was reluctant to take action. Think of a situation where your prospect would not explore his alternatives with you. Perhaps you could not get past the opening interview, into the factfinder. Often, the objection is unspoken. In this particular situation, did you recognize any of the problems your prospect was overlooking or ignoring? Probably! Remember, there are patterns. In most cases, we can see the problems more clearly than our prospects. We recognize these problems in just a few moments of conversation.

We can see it so readily, why can't they? This fog that surrounds their ability to recognize their own circumstances is called *denial*. Denial is most often a passive resistance to seeing reality.

Denial is a protective behavior that is used to suppress uncomfortable or unpleasant feelings. These feelings are usually the result of fear—fear of consequences, fear of the unknown. Haven't you ever dreaded something so much that you refused to even think about it? I certainly have. Our subconscious uses denial as a way to protect us from depression and ultimately death.

Most often, our prospective clients are so busy being successful that they just don't want to deal with issues they know need to be addressed. Can you think of any? Here are some to ponder.

- The client who has done his planning several years ago and knows the laws have changed.
- The prospect who knows that retirement is coming and hasn't started to set anything aside for income?
- The wealthy estate holder who has seen several estates decimated by taxes and hasn't taken the time to make any arrangements to protect his own estate.
- The business owner who knows he is nearing retirement and has not made any arrangements for successor management or business continuation.

The list is much longer than I could begin to detail. But the common denominator is always denial. They have an unwillingness to confront their problems primarily because they don't know if a solution even exists.

Sometimes they avoid issues because they are afraid of the cost. Other times they may be unwilling to exert the effort. It may be a hidden agenda about the ramifications associated with the solution. They don't want to deal with the black sheep, the alcohol, drugs or other family problems. They are afraid to tackle the underlying issues. Whatever the reason, the prospect is caught up in his denial and is often militant about even addressing it.

Ask yourself, what state of mind is your reluctant prospect in when you first come into his office. It probably would not come as a surprise that this prospect may not be a very good buyer at this moment. In fact, he probably will never really want to buy unless he can be emotionally moved from this place of denial to a place where his fear is replaced by desire—a desire to eliminate the issues and problems he faces.

It is difficult to feel confident sitting across from this prospect, who is anything but a "sparkplug of enthusiasm." So, what do we usually do? We attempt to make ourselves valuable by offering specific ideas and solutions to what we think are the most likely problems. After all, this strategy makes good sense. If the prospect hears something he likes, maybe he will "bite." The problem is that he may not be interested in hearing solutions because he is too busy denying he has any problems.

Herein lies the paradox of selling. The very solutions the prospect needs, which you have, are rejected because he doesn't *know* he needs the solution. Talk about a Catch 22. What is a person to do?

I believe salespeople can deal effectively with these prospects if they understand not only why people buy, but how they buy. Here is what I call the basic buying process:

The prospect starts in the *denial* phase. This occurs much the same way I described above. The pain of the problem is so great that the prospect suppresses any acknowledgment of its existence.

At some point, however, his denial comes to the surface and is replaced by what I'll call the *enlightenment* phase. The prospect moves from a place of ignorance to one of understanding. The light bulb goes on and he realizes there are some issues here he needs to consider. Let's not deal with how this happens, yet, but realize that when this occurs, you usually get positive feedback.

I think we salespeople are most vulnerable at this point. Our usual response is to start the "fixing" process. We bring out the charts, graphs, and illustrations in an attempt to become the hero by showing him how easy it is to fix his problem.

If the prospect is left to dwell on his new found understanding, then the next stage is the prospect's *recognition* of the *consequences* to the problem. Whether the consequences are a lower retirement income, the potential of forced liquidation of assets to pay taxes, or the sale of the business, the realization that the problem has a cost is crucial to the buying process. If the prospect is shortchanged in his ability to understand the consequences, the likelihood of making a sale diminishes significantly.

After the enlightenment and consequences phase comes the most important phase in the process—emotional acceptance. This phase could also be identified as the *grieving* phase. Once the prospect has been enlightened and the probable consequences are understood, the pain becomes apparent. The more it hurts, the more likely the prospect is to take some action, any action he can, to relieve the pain. In the recognition of this pain and the pricetag of fixing it (within his scope of knowledge) he grieves what he has lost by not planning sooner. The pain comes from realizing that he has very few alternatives and, if he doesn't take action, the pricetag will be much higher than he expected.

STEP   **1.**   **2.**   **3.**   **4.**

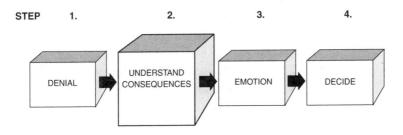

Once the prospect comes to grips with the reality of his circumstances, he becomes agitated and will want to remedy the problem. This agitation is the key to the sales process. It is a negotiation that begins with the pricetag of his current circumstances and works towards a preferred solution. The degree to which you are involved in this negotiation process will determine whether or not you can make a sale.

The fourth phase is *decide*. The prospect accepts his condition and wants to relieve the pain. He is willing to do whatever is reasonable to eliminate the pain. As salespeople, you need to be available with an action plan. This plan should accompany some type of decision path which allows the prospect to pick among appropriate choices. The lack of choice will usually postpone the decision and even drive him back to denial.

When the prospect becomes confused or feels he does not have enough information he becomes paralyzed. Paralysis results in procrastination. When people procrastinate, it is not because they are unable to make a decision. It is because they do not feel they have enough information to make the *best* decision. I have discovered most buyers want to make a decision and move on with their lives. But if they lose confidence in the process they will freeze. The salesperson's job is to keep the process moving. It will only stop when the buyer becomes confused or loses confidence in the process.

Now this may seem like psycho mumbo jumbo to you. But, if you can get past the words I am using and look at the feelings behind the issues, I believe this accurately describes the process everybody goes through when they are faced with tough decisions.

The buyer takes action because he believes the action will relieve the pain and solve the problem. As long as the pain feels worse than the cost, he will move forward. If the cost feels worse than the pain, he will not take action. Why fix something that is not broken? Most of all, why make it worse?

Defeating the Sales Process

As commission salespeople, we need our prospects to take action and take it soon. The longer people wait, the longer it takes for us to get paid. This can be quite painful. Our compensation system demands results. There is very little time to waste. We are trained to be expedient and move people through the buying process.

The temptation is to move people through this process too quickly. In fact, I have taken people through this process in one interview which culminated in what is called the medical close. The medical close occurs when the buyer decides to see if he can qualify for insurance. He writes the premium check when the policy is delivered. I was able to factfind, develop the problem, look at alternatives and then close by selling him on the best alternative, all in a matter of a few minutes.

However, the more complex the set of problems, the slower the process. When a fisherman hooks a marlin, the big game fish needs time to play out the line and become tired. Otherwise, the fish is too strong and you'll never get it into your boat. Smart fishermen know how to play the fish and work the process until they can land it.

So remember, allow the prospect enough time to assimilate the information and feel the pain. He needs to see clearly he has a problem and he needs to feel the consequences. Once the prospect understands, he will formulate the best solution from his own perspective and take action. If he chooses something other than what you recommended, it's likely you didn't clearly present your solution.

In the legal world, when a case is being prepared for trial, each side must go through the arduous phase of interviewing potential witnesses. This is called discovery. Well, we have a discovery phase too. It involves allowing the prospect enough time to work his way through all of the elements of his problem so that he can identify (on his own or with a minimum of help) what consequences he is up against. If you shortchange the prospect by cutting short his ability to experience the discovery process, you have undercut your chances in a couple of ways.

First, you have virtually eliminated the prospect's ability to grasp the full meaning of his situation. By moving too fast, you rob him of the opportunity to "own" the problem. This ownership requires that the prospect first discovers the scope of the problem and then believe that it is a problem. This is called "owning the problem."

For instance, a business owner who has not yet thought through the consequences of business succession, may not fully grasp the impact his death will have on his company. As a result, this owner may disregard any attempts to set up a business continuation plan or keyman insurance. Most advisors know a business faces severe economic and internal turmoil when it loses its leader. Loans may be called, suppliers may pull back credit and decision-making may falter causing cash flow problems. Whatever the problems, they are unique and yet the same.

The discovery process needs to focus on the survival strategies a company must implement when a key manager disappears. Ask the owner if he has ever known any businesses where the owner died or became disabled? Find out what happened. Develop his attitudes and thoughts about that situation. Ask what would happen if he were no longer there.

Sometimes he will demean his own value and say the company will be better off. But you need to stick with the pain and develop this further. Determine if what he says is really true.

You might say, "I hear you, but how many of your employees would feel comfortable working for this company if you were no longer here to solve the problems?" Put your statements and thoughts into questions that need longer answers than a grunt or moan. The prospect needs to come face to face with the possibility of death or disability. He needs to see that his death or disability could destroy their business. Most people will not want their life's work destroyed, especially if they can easily prevent it.

Likewise, a wealthy landowner, stockholder or investor needs to see clearly the impact of death on his estate. You need to help him visualize the possibility of losing 50-60% of his holdings. Ask him which assets would need to be sold. Ask what the sale of these assets would do to his portfolio. Would it make them feel like they did a good job of planning if 50% of their net worth were to suddenly evaporate, because of taxes.

Again, salespeople need to be known by the problems they solve, not the products they sell. When the focus is the product, then it becomes a commodity and becomes price sensitive. The buyer can become confused, and subject to multiple discussions of whose price is lowest. All of the features and benefits become less meaningful. The buying decision is often on the wrong issue.

When the focus is the problem, then the buyer is focused on the benefits and features. The price is important, but it does not dominate the decision-making criteria. As a result, the buyer becomes more rational and is based upon the appropriate factors, price being one of them.

A lack of trust occurs when you do not allow the buyer to process the discovery information properly. In the chapter on objections, you will find therre are four fundamental objections. The fourth one, No Confidence, occurs when the buyer doesn't feel ready or competent to make a decision. He distrusts because he lacks confidence either in his own ability to decide or in your ability to lead—either one is deadly to the sales process.

Besides the loss of confidence, another by-product of shortcutting the discovery process is the buyer's "loss of innocence." As mentioned earlier, when you first meet a prospect, he is usually in some stage of denial. The opening interview and factfinder are designed to bring the prospect through the denial process into enlightenment. Once he is enlightened, he must transition into the consequences mode. If he doesn't make this transition, he will return to denial.

Comments like: "I don't need to deal with this now," "the family will be all right if something happens to me," "the company can figure out a way to survive," are all denial statements. These statements indicate the prospect has little understanding of the problem and is unwilling to look closely at the consequences.

If we jump in with a solution too quickly, the prospective buyer will link the solution to the problem and will recognize the strategy the next time around. While there is nothing inherently wrong with this situation, the fear of taking action and the obvious bias that has prevented the prospect from taking action before, all come into play. The prospect, however, is now armed with limited information given out of sequence. This is where the "loss if innocence" occurs.

No good comes from "giving" the solutions away too soon. That's why you must learn to speak "consultation" and not speak "insurance" until the time is right.

Another problem that a proper discovery process overcomes is the paralysis of analysis. Once the prospect understands the scope of the problem and the limitations of his alternatives, it is easier for him to make a buying decision. If he feels there are other alternatives he does not understand or hasn't seen, his skepticism will "sink the ship."

As an advisor, you need to help the prospect discover his alternatives. By doing this, you gain his confidence and trust, but also maintain control of the process. If he learns his options from another source, you run the risk of losing the "most favored" position. If you are going to be faithful to your objective—to provide an ethical and complete array of choices—you need to fully explore all of the prospect's choices.

By now you should have an appreciation of what riskless selling is all about. The *perfect* sale is one where the buyer discovers his needs and selects your recommendation as the best solution. This can happen frequently if you are faithful to the process.

I believe the buyer must be brought through a process of understanding. This process starts with his denial and finishes with his desire. The closer you come to emulating this ideal model, the higher your probability will be of making a sale.

CHAPTER TEN

There Are No Magic Words

An objection is nothing more than an expression of the prospect's fear: his fear of being oversold, of being unable to pay for the coverage, of making an irrevocable mistake, or of buying from the wrong company or person.

I believe fear is the root emotion that underlies virtually every behavior. Fear also controls how someone directly or indirectly expresses his feelings. If you can discover what a prospect is afraid of, then you can help your prospect express his fear and ultimately assist him in overcoming it. If you ignore the fear, your prospect will not trust you and he will find another way to resolve the fear.

I have found most people are usually afraid of something. They may be afraid of failing, losing all of their money, retiring without an income, death, loss of children or spouse. There is no limit to what people can fear. Most people will not willingly admit they are afraid. They may be afraid to talk to anyone about what they fear. Sometimes they will be in total denial that they have any fear at all. Superstitions may play a role. Sometimes, they may believe that if they talk about their fear, it will actually happen.

Several years ago, my wife, Colleen, told me about an experience she had with our oldest son, Todd. He was 12 years old at the time and having a difficult time with his school work. Colleen went into his bedroom and found him not doing his homework as he had promised he would do. She became angry with him and let him have it with both barrels.

She later explained to me that her thought process went like this, "If Todd doesn't do his homework, he'll get a bad grade. If he gets a bad grade, he may fail the class. If he fails the class, he might fail out of school. If he doesn't get a good education, he won't get a good job or earn enough money to support himself. If he can't support himself, he'll starve. If he starves, he'll die." She was afraid that he would die. The anger had little to do with the homework and had everything to do with her fear of the ultimate consequence.

As I have thought about fear, I have come to believe that death is a core fear. In other words, at the heart of virtually every fear is the fear of dying. This fear may be for ourselves or for others. The fear of loss, the fear of rejection and the fear of death are the primary fears we face. However, I think fear of death is the dominant fear because there is absolutely nothing we can do about it.

If a prospect hides his real fear, then he is forced to use clever objections to hide the real fear. The lack of disclosure occurs when the buyer doesn't trust you or he doesn't fully understand the fear. This is why some objections seem so silly and absurd. It's important to remember that objections are really a mask to hide people's true feelings.

Understanding Our Role in the Sales Process

When I first started selling life insurance, I was taught that there are four basic objections: 1) no need, 2) no hurry, 3) no money and 4) no confidence. Virtually every objection can be categorized into one of these four areas. But basis of all objections is a lack of confidence. The prospect either distrusts you or he distrusts his own ability to make a good decision.

Your job in the sales process is to help prospects overcome their own fears by providing a safe environment for them to disclose their true feelings. In many cases, the real issue is simply a fear of making a mistake. If you can show that taking no action is a much bigger mistake and has more downside, the objection may disappear.

When I first started selling, I believed if I could get a "yes" or a "no," I had done my job. I saw my role as helping people make decisions. Today, I see my role differently. I want to help them do what they want to do. Why? If I have filtered this prospect properly and if I help him get what he wants, eventually, I will do business with him. Obviously, you would like the prospect to decide right now to buy what you are showing. But in sales, the way to survive is to rely on the law of large numbers. If you have enough good prospects, you treat them right, and you lay the proper the foundation, then I know you will do very well.

The law of large numbers says that if you have enough activity, some prospects will buy and some won't. If you strive to be perfect and sell everyone you meet, then ultimately, you have created your own *failure*. No one can sell everyone they meet, *unless the agent is so protective and restrictive that he only talks to people who know him and are going to buy anyway.*

As a facilitator, you need to adopt the attitude of a servant. Your job is to help buyers assess their needs and determine the appropriate solutions they should consider. If your product, insurance, can meet their objectives better than other financial alternatives, you have a sale. First and foremost, you should strive to help prospects understand their needs.

As a salesperson, you have two important tasks that you must accomplish successfully. You must understand the facts and then clearly establish with the buyer, his objectives.

> **If the facts and objectives are clearly understood and agreed upon, then an objection will no longer be an adversarial statement. It becomes a routine part of the sales process. It's not a war. Adversarial selling is a lose-lose proposition.**

I mentioned in a previous chapter my experience with a very successful senior level executive who indicated he was willing to help me. He had really wanted to understand my idea, so he was asking questions for information, but the questions appeared to be objections to my idea. I was defensive and reacted based on my fear. When he pulled me up short, I realized I had made an error in judgment.

Now this was an "aha!" Reasonable people try to understand what you are saying. Many times, what may sound like an objection is not an objection at all, but a question, an attempt to understand. Do you always know the difference? Ask yourself whether or not you assume threatening statements are always an objection.

Here is the footnote to that story about the businessman who called me on my defensiveness. Many years later the executive was the key decision-maker in what was probably the biggest life sale of my career—over $100,000,000 to one executive. I can guarantee you I wasn't defensive that time.

My point is, you need to discern between a true objection and an honest attempt to understand. A true objection is usually an expression of some fear. What should you do with someone who is afraid? How do you like to be handled when you are afraid? I like assurance and acknowledgment that my fear is valid and understandable under the circumstances. This assurance can go a long way toward resolving my fears. You cannot take away the fear, but you might be able to help the prospect determine the root of the fear, and maybe offer alternative ways of thinking that will help him resolve his concerns. If you cannot get beyond the fear, then the objection will remain real and the prospect is not likely to take action.

The most powerful skill you can develop as a salesperson/facilitator is to learn how to anticipate an objection. When you thoroughly understand the prospect's needs and attitudes, you should be able to evaluate his concerns. By offering the concerns before they become an issue, you can defuse the worry and the pain.

The Sales Process

Remember the sales process? Use the factfinder to determine and define the needs. Then design an array of solutions and model the costs. Present the models to the buyer and negotiate the best solution for him. Finally, you implement the sale. If you accurately anticipate the buyer's concerns during the process, the objection becomes part of the negotiation, the thinking process.

There is a basic rule of selling. *Whoever says the objection first, owns (or controls) the objection.* By this I mean, if the buyer goes on the offensive with an objection, you are placed in a difficult position. You cease being an advocate and consultant and you change roles—to a salesperson. This shift can be disconcerting for the buyer. He wanted someone who is going to comfort him and assist him in finding the best solution. You suddenly became an advocate for your solution. This incongruence will cause extreme distress and can void any trust that you may have built. If you suddenly shift to being adversarial, the shock could frighten the buyer away—back into denial.

By positioning major objections as a natural concern and using the objection as part of the education process, you are not adversarial. Rather, you are perceived as thoughtful and insightful.

Remember the "three circles of wealth?" One of the primary reasons for this story is the objection that wealthy business owners always use to protect their denial—the advisor. If you ask those questions during the filtering process and determine who they deal with and the extent they trust them, you are factfinding. If, however, they give you this information as a way to brush you off, it is a powerful objection.

Once the prospect says that he doesn't need this much insurance or doesn't want to spend this much money, you are in an argument. The prospect may be saying that he wants to wait, or that he wants to evaluate other alternatives. But by having to use it to push you away, he draws a line and dares you to cross it. A moment of truth has come into the process. Proper preparation and training allows you to postpone or perhaps avoid this moment of truth. Be prepared for these concerns and have a good answer ready. However, if you have done the correct job of positioning your presentation, objections become questions instead of a defense.

If a buyer says he doesn't need this much insurance, something went terribly wrong in the factfinding process. Where are the agreements between you and your prospect? What questions did he answer that led you to this recommendation? Where did I go wrong? What did I misunderstand? If the buyer has no money, is it because he didn't meet your profile originally? Maybe he is really unable to afford your recommendation. If so, where did the factfinding go wrong?

I hope you can see that these objections are only real if the factfinder you developed uncovered these issues. An objection should virtually never be a surprise. If it is a surprise, then something went wrong in the sales process. Let's say that your prospect has a good size company. You learn through your factfinding that the prospect has a lot of respect for the accountant and relies on him to help make these decisions. You need to meet this accountant and determine whether he is going to help you or hurt you. Offer to meet the advisor and ask him what issues and concerns he has for his client. Go over your thoughts and potential recommendations and ask for his input. By including the advisor in the planning process, he or she will find it very difficult to say no behind your back.

Early in my career, I learned this rule, "you don't have a case until you have a problem." In other words, expect the unexpected. But when it comes, remember that it is just part of the selling process. People will always have moments of regret as they deal with tough issues. You need to anticipate these problems. After a problem surfaces, it gives you a chance to resolve it satisfactorily and then make a long-term client out of the prospect.

A prospect may signal his unreadiness to make a decision by hesitating or procrastinating. But if you force him to move too quickly, you run the risk of ruining the relationship. By showing understanding and compassion, you signal a true concern for his needs and you strengthen the bond of trust.

If a prospect says, "I want to wait," you need to review the prospect's objectives and reconfirm your understanding of the prospect's goals. I might say, "What I am hearing you say is that you want to wait. Would you mind if I asked you a question? Based on the information you've given me, you seem to want to resolve this. Will waiting make this decision any easier for you? I've found that waiting makes it harder and usually more expensive to accomplish your objective."

By anticipating the objection, you are on the offensive instead of waiting for the objection that puts you on the defensive. Most of the sales material I have ever seen teaches the three R's: *repeat*, *reassure*, and *resume*. My goal is to penetrate and precipitate: penetrate the resistance and precipitate action.

You need to express your concerns by saying: "I sense that you" or "I believe, like you," or "If I were in your situation." I mentioned earlier that whoever expresses an objection first controls it. If you say the objection first, then your prospect can't take ownership of the objection. If the prospect says it first, he owns it and then must defend the objection.

The Four Objection Categories

I mentioned earlier in this chapter that there are four basic objections that underlie the fears of the prospect. Let's look at them and see if you can find the best way to deal with these common objections. Remember that lack of confidence is really the ultimate objection.

1. No Need. Typical "no need" objections include the following:

- My wife has a good education and can take care of herself.

- Her family will take care of her.

- I have a lot of cash in my investments and she can use this money to live on.

- She'll remarry, and besides, I'm not going to make anyone rich when I go.

- I didn't have anything when I started, therefore my kids can make it the same way.

- My partner can borrow the money from the bank.

The common denominator in these examples is selfishness. You must determine whether these objections are purely selfishness or a lack of understanding. I call the fear of facing the reality of death Denial. The only way to deal with it is to help the prospect understand the impact death has on a family and how easy it is to deal with the problem.

If you are dealing with selfishness, you may not have a prospect. Character is an important component of your profile. It is better to discover this early in the relationship than to wait until you have many hours invested with the prospect. If the problem is a lack of understanding, you need to go back and re-establish the basic strategies of the prospect in the factfinder. Did he really want to provide a guaranteed income? Was the college education really important? Can the partner borrow from the bank? Is that how the prospect wants to handle the problem if the tables were turned? If it is denial, then you need to establish the reality of death and the economic impact it will have on the family and the business.

For me, the "no need" objection is a strong signal I haven't done my job adequately. I must go back to the beginning and start over. I might say something like, "Bill, I really hear what you are saying. Obviously, if you believe your wife would be secure financially if you died, then I must have missed something. Tell me again how this is going to happen. Now this is the budget you showed me last month. Is this right, or did I misunderstand? Perhaps you could show me where the income is going to come from if you were to walk out of her life tonight. Is that what you want to happen?"

If the problem is not real, then the pain is not going to hurt. You must establish in the mind of the prospect a clear picture of the alternatives his family faces if he dies without planning. Ask whether or not the results you are forecasting are what he truly wants to leave as his legacy. Remember, we all are stewards of the resources we have been given. If we are bad stewards, usually our families suffer and strangers will benefit. Ask the prospect who he wants to suffer and who he wants to benefit!

2. No Hurry. No hurry means I can put this off for awhile, until I am more comfortable. Some "no hurry" objections include:

- Let me think about this issue, and I'll get back to you.
- I'd like to do this after I pay off my bills.
- I simply am unable to get to it yet; it's on the back burner.
- I'm too busy to take a physical right now, call me next month.

The "no hurry" objection is always an attempt to put off the inevitable. I have to be clear with these objections. I will often say, "Bill, I don't want to be the kind of salesperson who is so persistent that I become a *persona non grata.* If you want me to back off, just tell me and we'll forget this." Remember, you can't lose something you never had. You have to be able to fail to succeed. You have to be willing to lose to win. If you hang on too tightly, then you strangle the relationship. People are drawn to those who are strong, not those who are weak. You have to be willing to let go, to let people fall.

By giving the prospect room, most of the time the prospect will come back and say, "Oh, no! I still want to do this, but I can't right now." I then may ask the prospect to help me understand why. By letting the prospect talk, he will usually tell me how to sell him. Most of the time he will talk himself into it.

The key to the "no hurry" objection is for the prospect to tell you the next step. You need to get him to commit to something. When the prospect has agreed to commit, then you can go back and confront the prospect with his previous commitment. If the prospect says to call next month, I call and say, "Bill, you told me to call you at the end of the month. Well, I'm back!"

Eventually, the prospect either is going to buy from you or tell you to go fly a kite. If you have done the job right, then you eventually will make the sale if you are patient and persistent. The key is not to give up! Winston Churchill gave an eight word speech during World War II. He stepped up to the podium and looked out over the audience. He then said these famous words, "Never, never, never, never, never, never, GIVE UP." He then stepped down from the stage and left.

You only fail when you quit. The challenge is to know with whom you should sustain your effort. Make the prospect get rid of you. Don't throw in the towel and let the prospect off the hook. Never burn bridges! Let the prospect tell you he doesn't want to do business with you. Most can't or won't.

3. No Money. I think the "no money" objection is much easier to handle than the other two objections. Most "no money" objections are the result of doing a poor job of establishing the facts. If you have done a good job understanding the prospect's needs and financial situation, your recommendation should be solid and supportable. During the negotiation phase, the prospect ideally would have told you how much he can afford. If you believe that your recommendation is the right solution for your buyer, then you'll make the sale.

You can't ask the prospect to spend more than is reasonable. I believe "no money" just means he has no confidence in his ability to pay long term or no confidence in the decision he is making:

- I can't afford it right now.
- I'd just like to buy the cheapest coverage—term insurance.
- I'm unwilling to spend the money right now.
- I have to pay off my debts, first.
- I want to do it, but now is not the right time financially.

If you are looking for "magic words" to overcome sales resistance, they don't exist. People do what they want to do, regardless of what you say or think. There are no "magic words" that will suddenly turn chaff into gold. You cannot convince somebody to spend money he doesn't have. Buyer's remorse occurs when the prospect regrets his decision. If you have used "magic words," then it is likely the magic will wear off. The only real sale is one based on solid logic and an understanding of the relationship between the prospect's goals and the solution. If he doesn't want it, he won't keep it.

It's like the scales of justice. Somebody always wins and somebody always loses. Place all the reasons to buy insurance—debt payment, family income, college education, retirement—on the right side of the scale. Now place all the excuses and costs on the left side. If the excuses and costs weigh more than the benefits, the left side is heavier and the decision to not purchase wins the day. However, if the benefits are heavier than the costs, then the right side will be heavier and the buyer will buy. You must remember, people always do what they want to do when they want to do it. If the prospect doesn't want to buy, no amount of persuading will help the prospect change his or her mind.

The real underlying objection is no confidence. The previous three objections can be dealt with effectively by having a good profile and using good factfinding techniques when you build the relationship. But "*no confidence*" is at the heart of any real objection.

4. No Confidence. "No confidence" is usually a request by the prospect for more information. The common refrain of "no confidence" sounds like this:

- I want to shop around.
- I want to talk to my casualty agent.
- I want to talk to my accountant.
- I need more time to think about this.
- Are you sure this is the best thing for me to do?
- I need to talk this over with my partner.
- Give me a little time on this.

Most people find it very difficult to directly say no. After all, many people were raised to fear "no" and trained to say "yes." What do parents say when they don't want their child to do something? We are told to share with others and not to be selfish. We are taught that it is wrong to say no, and it hurts others when you are unkind and don't play fair. As a result, people learn manipulative techniques so they can get their way. They use objections that do not make any sense, but sound good to their ears. Your job is to make sense out of nonsense.

The first step is to articulate clearly what you think the prospect is saying. By repeating what you have heard, you assure the prospect that he has been heard. This is very important because too often the prospect feels discounted and is afraid he is going to be just another sale. Another benefit is that by repeating what he has said, he gets to hear his own words again and it enables him to evaluate if this is what he really meant. Penetrate the expressed concern.

For instance, I might say, "Bill, let's see if I heard you correctly. You don't want to increase your insurance because you believe your wife can pay the bills with her income. Is this what you were saying?"

It is important for the agent to remember that these objections are the prospect's way of saying, "You haven't convinced me yet." By dealing patiently with each objection, you establish your concern for the prospect. Sometimes I'll say, "I'm not certain I was clear with you about my concern."

If you brush off the objection, the prospect is likely to think you are more interested in making the sale than in helping the prospect to do the right thing. If Bill says, "I'd like to see how term insurance works," and you tell him that term is impractical, and callously return to your sales track, what will he do? Bill is going to get what he wants from another source.

Another thing for you to keep in mind is that objections are the prospect's way of telling the agent what he is thinking. If the prospect becomes entrenched in his position, you may be unable to help him see the advantages of your recommendation. This is why the ability to anticipate objections is so important.

The Value of Money

A sale is made when the prospect writes the check. This is the ultimate event. Helping the prospect determine how to pay the cost is the key to the sale. You must thoroughly understand the prospect's financial position. If the prospect has no money, you aren't going to be able to manufacture any. One of our best ways to build confidence is to show the prospect an effective and acceptable way to pay for the solution to his concerns.

In the life insurance world, premiums are capital. Sometimes it is difficult for the prospect to accept this premise. Although premiums do come from income, most often premiums represent savings dollars. I find the prospect will confuse premium dollars with his investment dollars. But investment dollars are capital at risk. Premium dollars are dollars for safety.

New money either comes from a person at work or from money at work. If the only dollars the prospect has, come from work, then you are probably talking about term insurance, unless you can demonstrate the need to start building capital for long-term investment purposes.

Money at work creates dollars to pay large premiums. It is merely a transfer of capital from one pocket to another, from one investment medium to another. If the prospect can understand that premiums are a way to leverage money, then permanent insurance will make more sense. If he only sees the premiums competing for other uses of his dollars, then it will be difficult to sell a large premium.

History supports the real value of money. Money replaced bartering. But money cannot earn a wage—only a person earns a wage with his effort and knowledge. Throughout the ages, money has only been worth 3%, plus a premium for inflation. If your buyer believes that money is worth 10% to 15%, then he is attributing an 8-10% additional value to the actual worth of the money. In essence, he is saying the money is worth too much and places too little value on expertise. The prospect must understand the risk before he will pay the price of the solution. When the prospect agrees that the solution is less costly than the problem, he will opt for the solution—insurance.

Objections are Part of the Process

I have been frequently asked what was the most difficult objection I ever faced and how did I handle it? The first one I recall happened in 1974. I had written a large life insurance policy to be placed in a pension plan. The company owner didn't like the idea but had agreed to have everyone take the physical to qualify. When I returned with the policies, he had changed his mind and didn't want the insurance.

My entire year was riding on this interview. It was December and I needed this sale to make my most important goals. When he said no, I went white. I felt defeated. I didn't particularly like this person and the process had been difficult. But I had the presence of mind to go back to the basics and start the sale again. We sat in the room for what seemed an eternity. When I finished rebuilding the sale, he agreed to buy the insurance and gave me a check. I always felt like I had forced him into doing something he didn't want to do. But I learned that an objection is difficult only if the agent *has* to make the sale. If I had had sufficient activity and had been independent from the sale, I could have been more removed, emotionally. No case should become so important that you can't afford to lose it.

Another example of how I dealt with objections predates the pension experience. This prospect was an orphan policyholder for the insurance company. My manager, Ralph, thought I should go call on him. Earl was a crusty old codger who owned and operated his own cabinet making shop. He didn't like insurance and he acted like he wasn't sure he liked me. My first visit caught him in the middle of a job and I stood by as he worked. I felt like the proverbial "penny waiting for change."

Finally, he stopped what he was doing and came over. We talked and I told him I thought I could help him. He gave me some facts and I could immediately see he needed more insurance. I was new in the business but I had enough presence to come back and show him some ideas. When I did, he responded with a nod and said he'd think about it.

After a time or two of dropping back to see if he had decided what he wanted to do, he finally said that it was too expensive for him. I had just learned about minimum deposit, so I suggested he look at using policy loans to pay premiums. He sent me back to do the calculations. When I came back, I got even more abuse as he ran me around and around on the concept and the numbers. After I had called on him for the eleventh time during the year, he finally agreed to buy. I had him examined, only to find that I now had to overcome some health problems to get him issued. Finally, I prevailed. The policy was issued standard and I placed the case. After he wrote the check, he put his arm around me and walked me out to the car.

"I decided I was going to buy from you the first time you came in to my shop. I just wanted to see you work for it."

We enjoyed a great friendship for many years. When Earl died, I delivered over $350,000 from all of the policies he had purchased through the years. The one I sold was the largest by fivefold. I always wondered what would have happened if I had given up. Steve Leimberg once told me that the difference between an old woman and an elderly lady is money. This client's wife died a few years later, but I know her life was better because I didn't let him scare me away. Have you ever felt that if they didn't buy from you, they might never buy at all?

THERE ARE NO MAGIC WORDS

You need to remember that objections simply are part of the sales process, but that you can make objections bigger than they really are. You must listen and evaluate what the prospect is really trying to say. Most often, the prospect merely is asking for help in understanding and overcoming the fear of making a mistake. If you look at an objection as anything other than a natural part of the sales process, you are giving the objection more power than it requires or deserves.

Remember that your role is to be the facilitator, to help your prospects assess their needs and determine if any of the financial products, especially insurance, will help meet their objectives. First and foremost, you must help them understand their risks. If you listen and help them evaluate their options, then you can build a relationship that will ultimately give them the confidence to do the right thing. After all, that *is* your job.

CHAPTER ELEVEN

Tying It All Together

If you have stuck with me through these pages describing my concept of sales consciousness, you have probably wondered how you can apply all of this in a practical way. After all, when you are in the "heat of the battle," so to speak, it is difficult to maintain your composure. But as we all know, it is often at this point in the selling relationship that the sale is made.

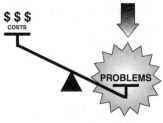

Remember, that we must be known by the problems we solve, not the solutions we sell. People are unwilling to take action unless they believe the problem warrants the cost. If we focus on solutions, we are forcing the client to acknowledge they have a problem. If we focus on problems, we are forcing the client to accept they need a solution. It is really that simple.

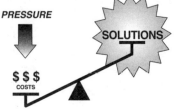

The way to accomplish this transition from solutions to problems is to develop a *selling process* that allows the prospective buyer to understand his problem and then decide whether or not the solutions he has readily available will work for him. I call this course of awareness on the part of the buyer the *buying process*. The ability to synchronize the buying process of the buyer and the selling process of the agent is an art and it is crucial to any successful strategic plan.

Let me summarize what I have tried to communicate for you in this book about the buying and selling processes—the basic components of a strategic plan.

The Strategic Plan

There are some very basic selling principles that have helped me establish a selling process but there is only *one* strategic plan. By tactically applying the basic principles, you can then follow your overall strategy and achieve your ultimate objective, personal satisfaction and plenty of sales.

Before reviewing the basic selling principles that make up the strategic plan, let's review the strategy itself first. Imagine a baseball manager going out to the ball park without a complete understanding of the skills and talents of each of his players. He knows each player's strengths and weaknesses and tries to manipulate the game situation to his advantage. He may order an intentional walk, a sacrifice, a stolen base or a hit and run. Regardless of his tactics, he has an overall game plan in mind. Like the manager, we must think strategically, too. We need to have a reason for everything we do, with an ultimate purpose in mind.

In this book, I have concentrated on how to discern whether or not you have a prospect, how to open a case and some issues to develop about in the fact-finding process. But most agents who have problems in the fact-finding process have difficulty because they are unable to tell the difference between a good prospect and a china egg. They waste time on prospects that they will never have a chance to sell. It is better to err on the side of productivity than to waste time with a prospect who might never buy. This is especially true during the beginning stages of your career.

I know this concept is likely to be controversial. Many sales trainers say that an agent should have as much activity as possible early in their career. But *perfect practice makes perfect.* Why not prospect a little harder and practice on buyers instead of non-buyers. It is pretty easy to sense who loves their family, who has character, who has a need, and who can afford to buy. Poor prospects are a result of fear. I have held on to bad prospects because I was afraid I would get no other prospects. Your ultimate strategy then is to start with the good prospect and from there apply the basic sales principles to the selling tactics in your selling process. You can achieve success faster by talking to successful prospects.

The Sales Principles

In order to effectively implement your sales process, think about the following sales principles I have already discussed in previous chapters. These principles cannot be ignored. You must learn them and trust them *before* you can apply them. A sales principle is nothing more than an observation about human behavior.

People do what they want to do, when they want to do it. We visited this one earlier in the book but do you believe it? If not, experiment and see how many people you can get to do what they don't want to do. Understanding this principle will set you free from guilt, shame, and blame. It will also release you from a lot of fears.

Whoever uses the objection first, owns it. An objection is either an appeal for more information or the prospect's way of telling you that you have not sold them yet. Either way, being complete in giving your prospective buyer all of the information they could ever need to make a decision is just good sense.

If you surface the issue and discuss it openly and honestly, you will be perceived as trustworthy. If you avoid the tough questions and hide from the issues, especially if you know they are going to be a problem, you are just kidding yourself. Be frank. Bring up the problem before they do.

People are too busy being successful. If ever there was a truth in selling, it is this one: people procrastinate because they don't want to take the time to focus and because they are afraid of making a mistake. As sales professionals, our job is to overcome this natural reluctance and develop a logical way for them to look at the issues. Being busy is the excuse they use to hide from the reality of their situation. Use their busyness to your advantage by making it the reason they need you. Take away the objection before they can use it on you.

Value-based selling. We are hearing a lot about this, but what does it mean? It means simply that buyers are going to be consistent with their pervious decisions. We need to help our prospects understand the inconsistencies that may exist between their beliefs and actions. It is a rare prospect that will not bring their overt decisions into parity with their values.

Sales Tactics

Once you believe these sales principles, you then must develop sales tactics in order to complete your strategy. Let's look at several tactics you can utilize to help you increase your effectiveness.

Have a selling process. Every successful seller has a pattern they have perfected, that works for them. Know your process and practice it regularly. Be so confident and bold in your process that you know you will always sell something. It is in this boldness that

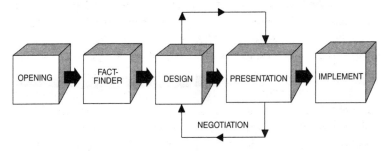

you can make the biggest impact in the lives of your clients. Understand the merits of what you sell and why people buy it. Work your process like an artist painting a portrait. Do everything on purpose and with confidence. The more you believe in yourself, the more the client will believe in you.

***Be known by the problems you solve, not the solutions you
sell.*** It is too easy to fall into the size 10 shoe mold. Be known for
your creative ideas, not for selling products. Be able to discuss the
problems your clients face in a non-product manner. Don't be
trapped into offering a solution before you know they are concerned
about the problem.

Make your sale in the factfinder. I hope by now you are convinced that the factfinder is where you allow the prospective client
to discover their problems and the consequences for themselves. It
is here you can delve into their mind and determine all of the pertinent data and values. You need to be able to show them how you
came up with your conclusions.

Develop a filter. A filter helps you protect your magic box. It
gives you a set criteria to use as a measure for all of your prospects.
If you are going to invest your time and resources in a prospect,
make certain the prospect fits your business model. Do things on
purpose. The first filter helps you determine whether or not you
want to do business with this prospect.

Develop a second filter. The second filter determines whether
the prospect wants to do business with you. Here you ask the simple
question, "Is there any reason why you can't do business with me?"
Eliminate everybody who
is not going to use your
services. Obviously they
cannot guarantee whether
or not they will buy, but
you can certainly find out
about any obvious rea-
sons why they will not
buy—like a brother-in-
law in the business, an

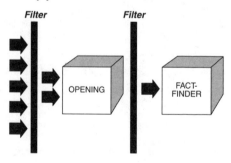

agent they already trust, or they don't do business unless their advisors agree. Whatever the reason, you need to negotiate the buying terms—*up front.*

TYING IT ALL TOGETHER

Recognize the buyer's process. Here we have probably the most subtle aspect of selling. *We* need to acknowledge the *buyer's rights.* The buyer needs to have time to process the importance of the decision they are making. Their process is one of understanding, price tags, acceptance, and decision. If we accept this process and manage our information process around their timing, we will be successful. If we fail to consider their timing needs, we are almost certain to fail in our attempts to do business with them.

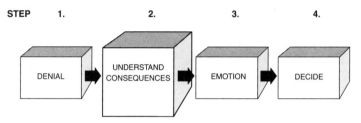

STEP   1.   2.   3.   4.

DENIAL → UNDERSTAND CONSEQUENCES → EMOTION → DECIDE

Don't be afraid to establish the rules of the game. Tell me the rules to the game and I'll tell you if I want to play. The buyer needs to know that you are serious about your relationship and that, as a business person, you are investing your resources into the relationship. When you negotiate the rules of the "buy," don't be afraid to tell them what you are doing. If they tell you they want to shop around, then find out how they plan to make the decision once they have all of the information. Make the buyer respect you and your business values. The more they respect you, the higher the probability they will do business with you.

Speak directly to their fears. If you have confidence and boldness, you can speak directly to their fear of what might happen. You may know exactly why they are not taking action but you back off because you are afraid to confront them. Speak directly to those fears. Raise the issue. Put it on the table. Then you can deal effectively with the issue and help them understand how your process can help.

Raise the issues before you show them solutions. A key to selling is to make certain you know everything you can, before you start to disclose the best solution. That's why the "I" word should not be used until the last part of the process. Once they know the solution, they can start coming up with all sorts of excuses. Remember, people will solve problems, but they don't buy solutions unless they have first bought the problem.

Don't use the "I" word too soon. This is probably the most important tactic you can adopt. Hold off using the "I" word until you are certain they understand the price tag of their problem and have emotionally internalized the cost. If you move too fast to solve their problem, they will not have processed it long enough to really want to do anything about it. Make certain they understand the price tag of their problem, before you show any solutions. Remember, whoever uses the "I" word first, loses.

Buying And Selling—The Strategic Plan

I have talked about the importance of understanding the buyer's process and the seller's process. When your selling tactics are implemented, they have to be used with an eye on the buyer's process. It is the buyer's process that really controls the flow and tempo of the sale. If you allow your own agenda to control the buyer's attitude, you run head to head against one of the basic sales principles— people do what they want to do. Helping them to do what they want to do is your strategic plan.

If people do what they want to do, then it is important to keep pace with their involvement. It may require an additional factfinding meeting. You may have to negotiate with them several times on the complexities of an irrevocable trust or a gifting plan. They must first buy into the liabilities of their plan before they will buy into the financing aspect of the plan.

I think we make a major mistake trying to get the prospect to understand the price tag of the solution too soon. It takes patience and skill to move a buyer through their buying process and end up at the decision point together. But when this is accomplished, great things happen. When we fail, it is a fiasco.

Matching the processes. Let's look at how the selling process and the buying process work together and our role, as the facilitator, in trying to time the outcome. Take a step back and think for a minute—what is our ultimate objective? Isn't it to help our client/ prospect accomplish what is in their best interest? I would think that in the final analysis if the prospect does what is best for them, then it will be best for us. Remember, people do what they want to do...

Having said this, there are two processes that are happening simultaneously. The buyer is processing the information and we, the sales person, are attempting to hold to a sales process that works. The objective is to make both arrive at the destination together.

Stages Of Buying And Selling. Look with me at the first stage of the buying process—Denial. Here we have a buyer who is unaware or unwilling to address important issues that relate to the financial well being of their family or business. The first two stages of the selling process, the opening and the factfinder are designed to awaken the denial. The buyer must respond to the stimulus or else we do not have a prospect. As a facilitator, we need to identify

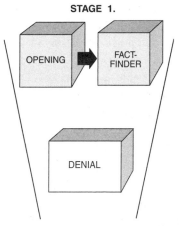

STAGE 1.

OPENING

FACT-
FINDER

DENIAL

the problem and then achieve a corresponding reaction. No reaction means no sale.

Assuming the prospective buyer responds, the second stage of the buying process is enlightenment and consequence. Here the buyer comes to the realization that they do indeed have a problem, and, better yet, they also begin to understand the price tag of their problem. The second stage of the selling process, the factfinder and negotiation, is aimed at helping the client come to grips with the scope of the problem and the magnitude of the solutions which are available to them. Without our intervention to help the prospect uncover the natural consequences, the price tag of the problem is predictable. Remember, every problem has a price tag and the prospect needs to be given time to process the problem and the related price tag consequences.

Stage three of the buying process is the emotional buy-in. I called this "grieving" earlier in the book. They have to assimilate the consequences and go through a process whereby they emotionally understand the severity of their circumstances and the lack of reasonable solutions to them. They need to

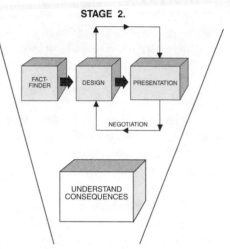

STAGE 2.

"feel" the problem. Our job is to help them through this process. The corresponding stage three of the selling process is the emotional bonding between you and the prospective buyer that takes place at this point. We become their confidant and friend. It is through this process that they learn to trust us and they see us as the

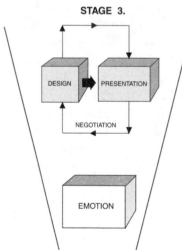

STAGE 3.

implementor of a solution. The problem needs to be seen in qualitative terms as well as quantitative terms. As long as this bonding is real and complete, you are virtually assured of making a sale.

The selling process needs to last long enough to allow the buyer to move through their buying process naturally. As the sales facilitator, we have to be aware of the progress our prospect is making through these stages and adjust the *tempo* of our presentation to accommodate their progress. The worst thing we can do is finish our process before the prospect has finished his. If this happens, you can be almost certain there will be no sale.

TYING IT ALL TOGETHER

Pacing Your Selling Process. Many sales people have learned to pace their presentation by experience and have come to a point where they do it without thinking. But I believe leaving this important strategy to chance causes many of us to fail under pressure. In golf, a player can shank a shot (hit it dead left or right because they fail to follow through) or yip a putt (lift up as they start to hit it.) These are signs of pressure and show up at the worst times. As professional salespeople, we need to have confidence in our "game." We need to know it will hold up under pressure. That's why understanding the buyer's process is so important. By recognizing each stage and pacing our presentation to our prospect's needs, we not

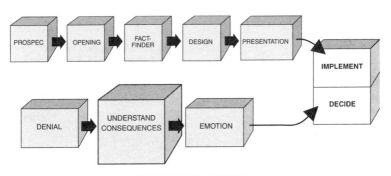

THE BUYERS PROCESS

only increase the probability of success, we also build lasting relationships.

The negotiation phase of the sales process is where we allow the buyer to process their grief. I do this by working through their issues in a series of well thought out iterations. An iteration is taking the plan design you have in mind and breaking it into smaller steps. Then introduce each step to the client as they become ready to move along the map you have drawn for them.

I must warn you this is tedious. But if you want to sell big cases, you must learn to do this or the only sales you make will be by good fortune, not necessarily sales skill. You have to pace the negotiation to match their understanding of the consequences and the emotional buy-in needed to make a decision to implement your suggestions.

Can you see why the "I" word becomes such a critical issue? Giving away the solution before the buyer is ready to consider alternatives shifts the focus from the pain of the consequences to the need for insurance. Then, the focus is on the wrong issue. You don't need to talk about insurance when the client is still thinking about whether they even have a problem. Until they understand their problem, there is no need for the insurance.

If you have paced the selling process properly, you arrive at the solution at the same time the buyer accepts that they have to do something. Masterfully orchestrating the timing of these processes can be as thrilling as hitting a home run in the bottom of the ninth or sinking a hole-in-one on the last hole. Having achieved this remarkable conclusion many times, I can tell you from my own experience, it is a wonderful feeling. There is joy in knowing you have done the job properly.

So now, the buyer wants to take action. They see the problem and understand that your solution is the ideal action. They want to solve their problem and they know there are no other acceptable alternatives. What greater testimony to the value of your service and experience is there than the satisfaction of knowing you have helped someone?

Why People Buy

So there you have it—*Why People Buy*. They buy because the facilitator has given them enough time to understand the dynamics of their situation and to face consequences without interference from you—the salesperson. In the psychobabble world, the need to interfere with this process could be called *codependency*. Our need to help others fix their problems is so great that we cannot stand to watch them agonize over the consequences of their situation. By interfering, we may temporarily become the hero but usually end up scaring the prospect away before the process is complete.

By waiting, we allow the progression of natural consequences to fall into place. We can influence the prospect's desire to deal with his circumstances. Once the prospect truly accepts the consequences and realizes the harm that could be done to the ones they love, they will do anything within reason to solve the problem and to remove the pain. Once they have had the opportunity to internalize that pain, they will buy to eliminate it. Your challenge is to trust this concept and apply it to your selling process.

Your Action Plan

1. Review your selling process. Do you have one? If not, develop one now before your next interview.

2. Develop a criteria for your future client base. Write down who you want to do business with and what common char acteristic they share.

3. Start now to match your prospect against your criteria. If they match, go sell them. If they don't match, then ask your self if you really need to invest your precious resources in them.

4. Develop a sensitivity to your buyer's process. Learn to recognize when they are in denial and when they begin to understand the problem and the consequences. Watch them go through the emotional buy-in and the acceptance.

5. Learn to pace your presentation to their process. Figure out how to turn your sales presentation into a negotiation—a back-and-forth fine tuning. Time your recommendation to coordinate with their acceptance that they must do something.

These five easy steps will bring you sales success. You can start now to build the practice you have always dreamed of having. You can reap the rewards of terrific referrals from happy clients. You can become the success you have always wanted to be. All you have to do is practice these concepts. Just remember, it is *perfect* practice that makes *perfect.*

HAPPY SELLING.